DOING BUSINESS IN THE UK

DOING BUSINESS IN THE UK

Opportunities and Pitfalls

Taylor Joynson Garrett

John Wiley & Sons
Chichester, New York, Brisbane, Toronto, Singapore

Published in the United Kingdom in 1995 by
Chancery Law Publishing Ltd
Baffins Lane
Chichester
West Sussex PO19 1UD

National (01243) 779777
International (+44) 1243 779777

Published in North America by
Wiley Law Publications
7222 Commerce Center Drive
Colorado Springs
CO 80919 USA

International (+1) 719 548 1900

Typeset in 11/13 Times by York House Typographic Ltd, London
Printed and bound in Great Britain by Biddles Ltd, Guildford and King's Lynn

ISBN 0471 956945

British Library Cataloguing Data

A copy of the CIP entry for this book is available from the British Library.

This book is printed on acid-free paper responsibly manufactured from sustainable forestation, for which at least two trees are planted for each one used for paper production.

CONTENTS

PREFACE

The information in this Guide was prepared by the professional staff of Taylor Joynson Garrett which is a law firm based in London, England. This Guide contains an outline of the major legal and commercial issues which will need to be considered by a foreign individual or company proposing to do business in England and Wales.

Many areas of law are changing with great speed. This Guide is not exhaustive and is based on the law as at 1 January 1995 with a few updating amendments introduced at proof stage in March. The information in this Guide is not exhaustive and is not intended to apply to specific circumstances. The contents of this Guide should not, therefore, be regarded as constituting legal advice and should not be relied upon as such. Accordingly professional legal advice should be sought before any formal action is taken as recommended in this Guide.

Taylor Joynson Garrett accepts no responsibility for any errors this Guide may contain whether caused by negligence or otherwise or for any loss howsoever caused or sustained by any person who relies on it.

If you have queries in relation to the contents of this Guide or require additional information, enquiries should be addressed to David Kent or any of the other partners in the International Corporate Group at the following address:

Taylor Joynson Garrett
Carmelite
50 Victoria Embankment
Blackfriars
London EC4Y 0DX

Tel: 0171 353 1234
Fax: 0171 936 2666

GLOSSARY

ACT	Advance Corporation Tax
BATNEEC	Best available techniques not entailing excessive costs
BS	British Standard
CAP	Common Agricultural Policy
CGT	Capital Gains Tax
DoE	Department of the Environment
DTA	Double Taxation Agreement
DTI	Department of Trade and Industry
ECU	European unit of currency
EEA	European Economic Area
EMU	Economic and Monetary Union
EPC	European Patent Convention
ERDF	European Regional Development Fund
ESF	European Social Fund
EU	European Union
FID	Foreign income dividend
GATT	General Agreement on Tariffs and Trade
HMIP	Her Majesty's Inspectorate of Pollution
HSE	Health and Safety Executive
IHQ	International Headquarters Company
IHT	Inheritance Tax
IPC	Integrated Pollution Control
LIBOR	London Inter Bank Offered Rate
MCPS	Mechanical-Copyright Protection Society
MCR	Merger Control Regulation
MTF	Merger Task Force
NIC	National Insurance Contribution
NRA	National Rivers Authority
OPR	Outward Processing Relief
PAYE	Pay-As-You-Earn
PCT	Patent Co-Operation Treaty
PLC	Public Limited Company
PPL	Phonographic Performance Ltd
PRS	Performing Rights Society
RES	Regional Selective Assistance
SFA	Securities and Futures Authority

SIB	Securities and Investment Board
SPC	Supplementary Protection Certificate
VAT	Value Added Tax
VPL	Video Performance Ltd
WRA	Waste Regulation Authority

USEFUL ADDRESSES

British Venture Capital Association
Essex House
12–13 Essex Street
London WC2R 3AA
Telephone: +44 171 240 3846

HM Customs and Excise
Advice Centre
Dorset House
Stamford Street
London SE1 9PY
Telephone: +44 171 928 3344

Department of the Environment
2 Marsham Street
London SW1P 3EB
Telephone: +44 171 276 0900

English Partnership
16–18 Old Queen Street
London SW1H 9HP
Telephone: +44 171 976 7070

European Commission
8 Storey's Gate
London SW1P 3AT
Telephone: +44 171 973 1992

Health and Safety Executive
Information Centre
Broad Lane
Sheffield S3 7HQ
Telephone: +44 114 2892345

Inland Revenue
Somerset House
Strand
London WC2R 1LB
Telephone: +44 171 438 6622

Invest in Britain Bureau
Department of Trade and Industry
Kingsgate House
66–74 Victoria Street
London SW1E 6SW
Telephone: +44 171 215 2501

London Stock Exchange
Old Broad Street
London EC2N 1HP
Telephone: +44 171 588 2355

Monopolies and Mergers Commission
New Court
48 Carey Street
London WC2A 2JT
Telephone: +44 171 324 1467

Securities and Investment Board
Gavrelle House
2–14 Bunhill Row
London EC1Y 8RA
Telephone: +44 171 638 1240

HM Treasury
Parliament Street
London SW1P 3AG
Telephone: +44 171 270 5000

See also page 35 for information on:

Enterprise Zones, Inner Cities, Regional Enterprise Grants, European Loans and Exchange Risk Cover, Loan Guarantee Scheme, Business Expansion Scheme, Derelict Land Grant, Enterprise Allowance Scheme, Training and Enterprise Councils

1. INTRODUCTION

Scope

Purpose of the Guide
Foreign investment in the United Kingdom
Introduction to Taylor Joynson Garrett

(i) Purpose of the Guide

This Guide contains an outline of the major legal and commercial issues which will need to be considered by a foreign individual or company proposing to do business in England and Wales. The contents of many of the chapters of this book apply equally to Scotland and Northern Ireland. However, the law in Scotland and in Northern Ireland can differ in varying degrees from that in England and Wales. In addition, court procedures and remedies are substantially different. In this Guide all references to the United Kingdom and to United Kingdom law are references to England and Wales and the law in England and Wales only, except where the text otherwise requires. If a foreign person is considering doing business in Scotland or Northern Ireland then legal advice should be sought from a firm of lawyers qualified to practice in those areas.

In the United Kingdom it is relatively easy for foreign corporations to commence or expand their business activities. The United Kingdom has always welcomed foreign investment. The completion of the European Union (EU) internal market programme and the elimination of barriers to trading goods and services between EU Member States means that the United Kingdom is an attractive location for expansion into continental Europe. A listing of the EU Member States is set out in Chapter 7.

This Guide has been prepared to provide a general overview of the considerations which will be of interest to a foreign business wishing to establish, acquire or expand a business in the United Kingdom or enter into a joint venture in the United Kingdom. It is intended to provide a summary of the basic law only and should not be relied on as providing legal advice. It is certainly not a legal textbook and makes no pretence that it is exhaustive on any subject referred to. Anyone considering doing business in the United Kingdom should obtain professional advice relating to their specific investment or activity and to the applicability of the relevant legislation to the particular facts.

(ii) Foreign investment in the United Kingdom

There are currently no restrictions on investment in the United Kingdom by overseas companies or foreign persons. There is no requirement in respect of UK companies that shareholders, directors or the company secretary be UK nationals. As from October 1979 all exchange control restrictions were abolished and accordingly profits from a business can be freely paid out to the foreign investor. The only restriction on such payments is the requirement to satisfy withholding tax obligations (see tax considerations).

The United Kingdom continues to attract high levels of inward investment from companies from all parts of the world. The government actively encourages overseas investment, recognising the many benefits it brings to the UK economy. For example, in the thirty years from 1951–1991, 36% of US foreign investment and 40% of Japanese foreign investment was in the United Kingdom. This is represented by the existence of over 3,500 US firms present in the United Kingdom and over 180 Japanese firms, including all 10 major consumer electronics firms.

It is not only the United States and Japan that have invested heavily in the United Kingdom. Virtually all European multinationals have established operations, including over 1,000 German companies.

The UK business environment benefits from the following governmental assistance (see Chapter 3):

- lowest main corporate tax rate in Europe;
- no exchange controls on profits sent overseas;
- 100% allowances on trade-related research;
- competitive labour costs;
- use of English as the "world" language.

(iii) Introduction to Taylor Joynson Garrett

Taylor Joynson Garrett is a top London law firm with 64 partners and a total of around 400 staff. The firm provides a full corporate law service and specialises in corporate law, securities and banking law, litigation, real estate law, and tax and personal planning. In addition, the firm is ranked as one of the premier UK firms in intellectual property law (the law relating to patents, copyrights, trademarks and other related rights).

Taylor Joynson Garrett meets clients' needs by combining the skills of individuals from across the firm to form practice groups which deal with problems in specialist areas. Amongst the key practice groups are:

- banking/insolvency
- banking litigation
- biosciences
- company
- construction
- contract and commercial
- corporate finance
- corporate fraud
- energy
- entertainment
- environmental and natural resources
- European Union
- financial services
- food & product labelling
- franchising
- immigration & labour
- insurance

- information technology and multimedia
- international trade
- litigation
- patents
- publishing
- real property (real estate)
- shipping
- technology transfer
- trademarks and anti-counterfeiting

The majority of the practice groups consist of lawyers from both non-contentious and contentious sections of the firm.

International network

In order to provide a comprehensive service for clients with international businesses throughout the world, we have adopted a four tier approach.

Brussels Our Brussels office advises on all aspects of European Union law and its impact upon the conduct of business throughout the EU.

Romania Our Romanian representative office advises clients investing into or trading with the former Eastern bloc.

International affiliations Affiliations have been established with a number of leading law firms covering all the major trading nations. Together the firms form one of the largest international groups, with over 1,000 lawyers.

The firms co-operate in representing clients with multi-national business interests from all the main economic areas of the world. We recommend each other as counsel of choice although, naturally, clients can make their own selection if they prefer. A number of world-wide practice groups have been formed which meet regularly to discuss legal and business developments in the various jurisdictions. Our international affiliations give us the ability to provide our clients with a focused and consistent service by involving local lawyers with proven expertise.

Interlex Taylor Joynson Garrett is also a founder member of Interlex, a more informal association of independent law firms which has been established since the early 1970s in over twenty countries.

Services to international clients

Taylor Joynson Garrett's international corporate group works with the firm's various practice groups. This group specialises in working for businesses of all sizes which are setting up and doing business in the United Kingdom and Europe. The group comprises 14 partners organised in informal country desks and taken from various specialist practice areas within the firm. Each partner has two associates assigned to him who work with the partner on matters for his overseas clients.

Taylor Joynson Garrett's international group prides itself on understanding its clients' needs for quality and responsiveness and for all relevant parties to be kept informed at all times. It is this responsiveness and these communication skills which ensures that the group does not undertake unauthorised work. This experience comes from many years of working with overseas multinationals.

2. FORM OF BUSINESS ORGANISATION

Outline An overseas company may carry on business in the United Kingdom through a subsidiary company or through a branch of the overseas company registered in the United Kingdom. In addition an overseas company can establish a limited presence in the United Kingdom under the place of business registration scheme. Business activities may also be conducted through a sole proprietorship, a partnership or a joint venture. Goods and services may be supplied through contractual arrangements such as distributorship agreements and agency arrangements without actually setting up business in the United Kingdom. The legal implications of the respective methods and vehicles are summarised below.

Scope

Company law
Choice between branch and subsidiary
Formation of a subsidiary company
Branches of overseas corporations
Place of business registration regime
Partnerships
Joint ventures
Sole proprietors
Insolvency
Distribution and agency arrangements

(i) Company law

Both subsidiary companies, branches and places of business are currently regulated by the Companies Act 1985 (as amended by the Companies Act 1989).

Companies incorporated in the United Kingdom can be private or public. Public companies must however meet certain requirements:

- the company's authorised and issued share capital must be at least £50,000;
- the memorandum of association must state that the company is a public company;
- the name of the company must include the words "public limited company" or "PLC";
- the Registrar of Companies must have authorised the company to commence business.

Private companies unlike public companies need not meet the above requirements but may not offer their shares or debentures to the public.

Private companies may have limited or unlimited liability or may be limited by guarantee (without a share capital). If a company's liability is limited the word "limited" or "ltd" must be included in its name.

(ii) The choice between branch and subsidiary

(a) Taxation

Both a branch and a subsidiary will be liable to corporation tax on taxable profits including a proportion of capital gains. However a subsidiary will be liable to account for Advance Corporation Tax ("ACT") on all qualifying distributions, whereas a branch will not have to account for ACT on remittances to its parent. The liability to account for ACT does not necessarily increase the amount of corporation tax payable by a subsidiary, although there will be a timing disadvantage for the subsidiary as compared with a branch.

Losses of a branch may be available for release against the overseas company's own profits in its territory of residence.

A subsidiary as a resident of the United Kingdom is entitled to a credit for non-UK taxes whereas a branch would only be entitled to treat non-UK taxes as an expense.

It may be more difficult for the deduction of interest to be allowed for a branch as compared with a subsidiary, although a non-discrimination clause in the relevant double taxation treaty may alleviate the disadvantage.

The subsequent conversion of a branch to a subsidiary (or a subsidiary to a branch) will represent a disposal for capital gains purposes of all relevant assets transferred, which in addition to tangible assets such as freehold and leasehold property, will extend to intangible assets such as goodwill. However capital gains tax deferral relief can now be obtained if both the overseas company and the subsidiary make a claim within two years after the end of the accounting period of the subsidiary during which the disposal was made.

Where the non-UK resident company is resident in a country which has a double tax treaty with the United Kingdom which entitles it to a tax credit on dividends from the UK subsidiary this may reduce the effective rate of UK tax on distributed profits. In some cases this may make a subsidiary the most tax effective vehicle to be used. However specific professional legal advice will be needed in each circumstance.

(b) Legal existence

A branch office of an overseas company will be part of the overseas company with no separate legal existence.

A UK subsidiary of an overseas parent company will have a separate legal existence from the parent company, thus the parent company will not be liable for debts or the subsidiary's obligations beyond the amount of the subsidiary's share capital, unless the parent company were to give an express guarantee or indemnity. On the other hand since a parent company is not liable for its subsidiary's debts, a subsidiary which is a private limited company must rely on its own credit worthiness, which will depend at least initially on the share capital paid in by its parent. The paid up share capital of a private limited company cannot be withdrawn except by order of the court or following the subsidiary's liquidation.

This can be compared with the situation with a private unlimited company where the paid up share capital can be withdrawn by a shareholder's resolution. Private unlimited companies can be useful in repatriating losses to US corporations as they are capable of being treated as unlimited partnerships under US tax law. However, a private unlimited company does not limit its shareholders' liabilities in the event of insolvency.

(c) Filing requirements

If the overseas company establishes a branch in the United Kingdom, the information to be registered (see below) will include filing the overseas company's accounts in the form required of a UK company (except that this rule is never enforced) with the Registrar of Companies both on the setting up of the branch and annually thereafter.

A subsidiary company will be required to file its own accounts and certain other information with the Registrar of Companies each year. It will also need to identify the overseas company as its ultimate parent, but beyond that no information need be given about the parent.

Practical point

Compliance with filing requirements, particularly in respect of the accounts of the overseas company is a substantial factor for many overseas companies and often results in the decision to form a subsidiary so as to avoid the need to file the overseas company's accounts.

(d) Service of legal proceedings

If the parent company establishes a place of business in the United Kingdom it must appoint some person in the United Kingdom to accept service of legal proceedings on its behalf. This makes it easier to bring legal proceedings against it in the English courts in respect not only of matters relating to the UK branch but also of matters relating to the head office or other branches of the parent. By contrast the incorporation of a UK subsidiary does not make the parent company liable to legal proceedings in the United Kingdom.

(e) Other factors

An advantage of a subsidiary is that, because it is set up in the normal UK form for companies, its administration is easier and its position more readily understood by those with whom it does business than is the structure of a branch. A further disadvantage of a branch is that it cannot take advantage of certain UK Government schemes which are available to UK subsidiaries, such as export credit guarantee facilities.

(iii) Formation of a subsidiary company

(a) Introduction

The mechanics of setting up a UK subsidiary are relatively simple. A company can be acquired "off the shelf" and the name of the company can be changed to incorporate the name of its parent, assuming that there is not already another company registered with the same name. Care also needs to be taken to check with the Trademarks Registry to ensure that the company name will not infringe a third party's trademark or result in a passing off action. Alternatively a tailor-made company can be incorporated.

A private limited company:

- in accordance with the Companies (Single Member of Private Limited Companies) Regulations 1992 (see (b) below) may be formed by one person and may have only one member;
- but otherwise must have at least two officers (a director and a company secretary). In practice it is usual to appoint at least two directors. There is no requirement that an officer of the company is a UK national;
- must have a registered office address at which the statutory books of the company should be kept.

Practical point

The process of changing the name of a company usually takes ten days from receipt of the necessary documentation by the Registrar of Companies. If a UK company is required as a matter of urgency it is possible to obtain a shelf company and then register the change of name on a same day basis on payment of a fee (currently £200).

(b) Single member private limited companies

Where a private limited company has a sole member and the sole member is also a director of the company, the terms of any contract entered into by the company with the sole member must, unless the contract is in writing, be set out in a written memorandum or recorded in the minutes of the first meeting of the directors of the company following the making of the contract. This does not apply to contracts entered into in the ordinary course of the company's business.

If the number of members of a private limited company falls to one, a statement that the company has only one member (together with the date on which the company became a company with only one member and the name and address of the sole member) must be entered in the company's register of members. Likewise, if the membership of a company increases from one member to two or more members, a statement that the company has ceased to have only one member (together with the date on which that event occurred) must be entered in the company's register of members, with the name and address of the person who was formerly the sole member.

Notwithstanding anything in the company's articles, the quorum for members' meetings in respect of a company with a sole member is one.

Where a sole member takes a decision which may be taken by the company in general meeting and which has effect as if agreed by the company in general meeting, the member must provide the company with a written record of that decision (unless the decision is taken by way of written resolution);

The provision in section 122 (1)(e) of the Insolvency Act 1986 (*i.e.* that a company may be wound up by the court if the number of its members is reduced below two) has been amended so that a private limited company is excepted from this provision.

(c) Particular issues

Specific matters which must be considered on incorporating a subsidiary company are as follows:

Company identification

Every company must ensure that its name is stated in easily legible letters on the outside of every office or place in which its business is carried on. In addition, its name, place of registration, registered number and registered office address must appear on all business correspondence and other publications.

Practical point

It is common practice to include the company's VAT number on all stationery, publications, etc of the company but this is not required by law on correspondence. However, it must be included on invoices.

Accounts

Each private limited company is under a duty to keep proper accounting information, set an accounting reference date, and to have its accounts audited (unless the company is dormant). The company must then forward copies of the audited accounts to the shareholders (or lay such accounts before the company in general meeting), and file the audited accounts with the Registrar of Companies. The content and format of the audited accounts is regulated, but smaller companies may file less detailed unaudited accounts. Accounting reference periods are usually 12 months, although a company may, in certain circumstances, alter its accounting reference date. An accounting reference period can never be longer than 18 months.

Annual return

Every year, a registered company must submit an annual return in the prescribed form, signed by an officer of the company. This annual return must include certain specified information, for example, the address of the registered office, the type of company and its principal business activities, the name and address of the company secretary and every director together with details of the nationality, date of birth and business occupation of each director.

Failure to file annual returns or accounts punctually may lead to the UK Registrar of Companies taking steps to fine the company and its directors and eventually to strike the company from the Register. This will have the effect of terminating the existence of the company and vesting all its property in the Crown.

Practical point

Following a striking off it can be an expensive exercise to apply to the court to place a company back on the Register for the purpose of making a valid transfer of its assets out of the company.

Register of members

Every company is under a duty to keep a register of its shareholders (known as "the members" of a company). This register must include the names and addresses of shareholders, the number and class of shares held and a record of the date when the person concerned first became and subsequently ceased to be a member of the company.

Register of charges

Every company is under a duty to keep a register of charges (security interests) granted by it over all or specified parts of its property or undertaking. It is also incumbent on a company to register the details of these charges with the UK Registrar of Companies, failing which they will be unenforceable.

Auditor

Unless a company is dormant throughout an accounting reference period (*i.e.* no significant accounting transaction has occurred throughout that period), a company must appoint an auditor. This obligation is qualified by the Companies Act 1985 (Audit Exemption) Regulations 1994 and the Companies Act 1985 (Audit Exemption)(Amendment) Regulations 1994 which allow for "small" companies to take advantage of certain audit exemptions in the preparation of their annual accounts. Only private limited companies **which are not subsidiaries or parents of other companies** qualify for these exemptions, and banks, insurance companies and other financial institutions are excluded. Further, to meet the qualifying criteria, the company must have an annual turnover of not more than £350,000 and a balance sheet total of not more than £1.4 million. The exemptions relate to the requirement to have annual accounts audited.

If the company qualifies, it may prepare unaudited accounts without a directors' report or a profit and loss account. It must, however, prepare a balance sheet although this would be in an abbreviated form. Various statements must be included in the balance sheet which reflect the exemptions which are being claimed by the directors. Although the accounts are not audited, the accounts must be accompanied by an accountant's report which comments on whether the accounts are in agreement with the company's accounting records, whether they have been drawn up in a manner consistent with the provisions of the Companies Act 1985, and whether, on the basis of the information contained in the accounting records, the company qualifies for the exemptions claimed by the directors. A company with a turnover of less than £90,000 does not require this accountant's report. None of the exemption provisions prohibit the company from preparing full audited accounts.

The legislation lays down qualifications for a person to be appointed as an auditor (basically an accredited accountant).

Accounting reference date

The Registrar of Companies should be notified of the company's accounting reference date and this is likely to be the same date as the parent company. Notification should be given within nine months of the company's incorporation date, otherwise the Registrar of Companies automatically allocates the company's accounting reference date, which is the last day of the month on which the anniversary of its incorporation falls.

Financing

It will be important to decide how much the share capital of the UK subsidiary should be and the extent to which it should be financed by debt. The level of share capital will be largely dictated by commercial requirements, but there are two other factors to consider:

- *Credibility*
  This is largely a matter of how the company appears to others: potential customers, clients and its competitors. Generally speaking the larger the issue of share capital the greater the credibility factor. Although there are no hard and fast rules it would be advisable to consider an issued share capital in excess of £1,000. This may necessitate increasing the authorised share capital if the

sum decided is in excess of £1,000 but this can be done very simply by a members' written resolution. If the authorised share capital is increased the company will probably wish to increase it beyond the proposed issued share capital so as to give some flexibility as regards issuing further shares in the future.

- *The implications of debt finance (thin capitalization)*
  If the parent company is considering some form of interest-bearing loan to its UK subsidiary, it should consider the detailed rules which the Inland Revenue apply to payment of interest by a UK company to an overseas parent. If the UK company has a small amount of equity capital compared to the amount of debt, the Inland Revenue may deem the interest paid as a distribution on which the UK company would not be entitled to a tax deduction and on which it would be liable to pay Advance Corporation Tax (as if the interest were a dividend). The general rule is that the proportion of interest bearing loans from its parent, to its paid up equity share capital, should be in the proportion of 1:1.

The Companies Acts regulate a large number of issues other than those outlined above, for example:

- internal management/powers/authorizations/rules of meetings;
- the adoption and use of corporate names;
- the maintenance of capital (including the prohibition on the company giving financial assistance in connection with the acquisition of shares in the company);
- the enforcement of fair dealing by the company's directors (for example, governing transactions between the company and its directors, the prohibition – with minor exceptions – of loans by the company to directors, the duty of directors to report shareholdings in the company and associated companies and the duty of the company to keep a register of such shareholdings);
- the investigation of the company's affairs by the Department of Trade and Industry.

Company names

The Registrar will not accept for incorporation a company with the same name as a company already on the register. In addition, names including certain specified words or expressions will not be acceptable. Certain words such as "International", "Royal" and "British" may be included in a company's name only with the prior approval of the Registrar of Companies. The names that require approval are set out in the Business Names Regulations 1981 (as amended). Care should also be taken that the chosen company name does not infringe a third party's trademark.

Directors' duties

Every director of a company owes certain duties to the company's shareholders, employees and creditors under both common law and statute, which, if breached, could result in personal liability. Professional advice should be taken before any person agrees to become a director. The Institute of Directors also provides helpful booklets on this subject.

(iv) **Branches of overseas corporations**

(a) Introduction

The rules governing branches and the presence of overseas companies in the United Kingdom (except subsidiaries) have recently been amended by the Overseas Companies and Credit and Financial Institutions (Branch Disclosure) Regulations 1992. These regulations introduce a branch registration scheme which complies with the EU Eleventh Company Law Directive 89/666/EU and the EU Bank Branches Directive 89/117/EU. The Companies Act contains two regimes which regulate the registration of an overseas company in the United Kingdom – the branch registration regime, and the place of business registration regime.

(b) Distinction between branch and place of business

A limited company incorporated outside the United Kingdom and Gibraltar which opens a branch in the United Kingdom is required to register in the United Kingdom under the new scheme. Under English law a branch is regarded as part of the overseas company, and will be organised so as to conduct business on behalf of the overseas company. This means that a person will be able to deal direct with the branch in the United Kingdom instead of with the company in its home country. The term "branch" is used in a sense close to the concept of a subsidiary, although the main distinction is that it will not be a separate corporate body. It may, however, operate from a number of locations within the common management structure of the overseas company.

In general a place of business will not amount to a branch if the business carried on at that place is only ancillary or incidental to the company's business as a whole. Examples of such operations include warehouse facilities, administrative offices and registration offices for the overseas company.

(c) Procedure for branch registration

An overseas company which has opened a branch must within one month of doing so deliver to the Registrar of Companies the particulars of the **overseas company** on form BR1 as follows:

- the corporate name of the overseas company;
- if registered in its country of incorporation, its registration number and the identity of the register;
- its legal form, *i.e.* public or private company;
- a list of its directors and secretaries;
- the extent of the authority of the directors to represent the company in dealings with third parties and in legal proceedings, together with a statement as to whether they may act alone or must act jointly and, if jointly, the name of any other person concerned;
- whether the company is a credit or financial institution; and
- if the company is subject to any winding-up or other insolvency proceedings.

In addition, if the company is not incorporated in a Member State of the European Union the company must state the law under which the company was incorporated, the address of its principal place of business in its country of incorporation, the company's objects, the amount of its issued share capital, its accounting reference date, and the time allowed under its parent law for preparation and disclosure of accounts.

In respect of the **branch** the following particulars must be given:

- address;
- date on which it was opened;
- business carried on by the branch;
- name in which that business is carried on, if different from the name of the company (but see (iii)(c) above);
- names and addresses of all persons resident in the United Kingdom authorised to accept service on behalf of that company in respect of that branch;
- names and usual residential addresses of all persons authorised to represent the company as permanent representatives of the business of the branch; and
- extent of the powers exercised by the persons listed above.

The company is also required to file a certified copy of the instrument defining the constitution of the company (including, if necessary, a certified translation).

(d) Letterhead

An overseas company which has registered a branch must:

- display the company's registered name and its country of incorporation at every place where it carries on business in the United Kingdom;
- state the company's name and country of incorporation on all stationery, notices and other official publications of the company;
- if the liability of the company's members is limited this must be stated on all stationery, notices and other official publications and displayed outside every place of business; and
- state on all letterhead and order forms the place of registration and registration number of the relevant branch.

In addition, if the company is not incorporated within the EU, and is required to be registered by the law of the country in which it is incorporated, it must state on its letterhead and order forms used in the business of the branch the place of registration of the parent company and its registration numbers, together with the legal form of the company, the location of its head office and, where applicable, the fact that it is being wound up.

Practical point

Sample branch letterhead for a non EU overseas company should include this information:

XCo Inc
[UK address]
Registered in England under branch No ZZZ
HEAD OFFICE ADDRESS: [ ]

A US corporation registered
[with limited liability]
in California under No XXX

(e) Disclosure of annual reports and accounts

Where disclosure of annual reports and accounts is required in the state of incorporation of the overseas company which is registered as a branch, it must deliver for registration with the other documents required to be delivered upon registration of the branch, copies of its latest accounting documents prepared and disclosed in accordance with that law. Where the company is not required to make public disclosure of its accounts, it is required to prepare and deliver accounts in the same manner as a company subject to the place of business regime (*i.e.* in a form not as detailed as is required if the company were incorporated in the United Kingdom, and the accounts do not need to be audited). Directors reports are not required, nor is disclosure of details of directors' remuneration, loans or similar transactions. A balance sheet and profit and loss account showing comparative figures for the previous year are required.

Thereafter accounts must be delivered to the Registrar within thirteen months of the accounting reference date.

(v) Place of business registration regime

If an overseas company has established a place of business in the United Kingdom it must deliver to the Registrar of Companies within one month of establishing that place of business a Form 691 which includes details of the company's directors and secretaries, details of the name and address of persons authorised to accept delivery of documents on the company's behalf, a statutory declaration stating the date on which that place of business was established, and a certified copy of the charter, statute or memorandum and articles, or other instrument which defines the overseas company's constitution.

The company is required to deliver in respect of each financial year copies of its reports and accounts prepared in accordance with the Oversea Companies (Accounts) (Modifications and Exemptions) Order 1990, which means that the accounts do not need to be as detailed as those required if the company were incorporated in the United Kingdom, nor do they need to be audited. Directors' reports are not required, nor is disclosure of directors' remuneration, loans or similar transactions. A balance sheet and profit and loss account showing comparative figures for the previous year are required.

The overseas company must display the company's registered name and its country of incorporation at every place where it carries on business in the United Kingdom, state the company's name and country of incorporation on all letterhead, stationery and notices and other official publications of the company, and if the liability of the company's members is limited, state that fact on its stationery, letterhead and notices and other official publications of the company and display it outside every place of business.

Practical point

A place of business registration is appropriate when the overseas company performs functions in the United Kingdom that are only ancillary or incidental to the company's business as a whole, *e.g.* warehouse facilities.

The company must notify the Registrar of its corporate name when it establishes a place of business in the United Kingdom. The names of overseas companies are subject to the same regulations as companies incorporated in the United Kingdom and it may be that the corporate name of the company is not acceptable or is permissible only with the approval of the Secretary of State for Trade and Industry. If the company's name is unacceptable the company may be required to adopt a business name for use in the United Kingdom. A trade mark search should also be conducted (see (iii)(c) above).

(vi) Partnerships

The rights and obligations of partnerships are governed by partnership agreements and by the Partnership Act 1890. As a general principle, partners are not only jointly liable to creditors for the debts and obligations of the partnership, but each partner is also personally liable for all the debts of the partnership not satisfied by the partnership assets (joint and several liability). A partnership may not consist of more than twenty partners, with certain exceptions, including lawyers, accountants, members of a recognised stock exchange, and other purposes specified by the Department of Trade and Industry. There is no requirement that all or any of the partners should be UK nationals, and a company may be a partner.

It is possible under the Limited Partnership Act 1907 to incorporate a partnership which has one or more general partners who manage the firm's business and have unlimited liability, together with one or more limited partners who are not liable for the debts and obligations of the partnership beyond the amount of the capital which they invest in the firm.

Disclosure requirements for partnerships are minimal. If the partnership has a place of business in the United Kingdom, and its name does not consist of the surnames of all the partners who are individuals, and the corporate names of all partners who are corporations, all stationery must show the names of the partners of the firm, subject to the exception of partnerships of more than twenty persons. All stationery must also show a business address. This information must also be displayed at all business premises of the firm.

Practical point

A partnership is unlikely to be a vehicle for inward investment in the United Kingdom.

(vii) Joint ventures

A joint undertaking is generally organised either as a partnership or through a jointly owned company. The relationship between the joint venture parties is usually governed by a joint venture agreement or by a subscription and shareholders agreement, negotiated between the parties, and which sets out their respective rights and obligations.

Practical point

These are complicated arrangements requiring much thought and negotiation, particularly as to what happens if the parties fail to agree on any course of action. The EU competition rules may also apply and professional legal advice should be sought.

(viii) Sole proprietors

Individuals including non-UK nationals may do business in the United Kingdom as sole proprietors. There is no limited liability for sole proprietorships and the personal assets of the sole proprietor will be at risk in respect of any obligations of the business.

(ix) Insolvency

The Insolvency Act 1986 (and associated rules) governs the winding-up of companies. In several instances, the legislation can have retrospective effect, and directors in particular need to be aware of its provisions during the life of a company. Not surprisingly, there are many provisions which impose sanctions on company officers whose activities are exposed in the course of a liquidation as having been fraudulent. Potential personal liability of directors may also be incurred where there has been no fraud but there has been "wrongful trading". This applies if the company has gone into insolvent liquidation and at some time before the commencement of the winding-up of the company, a director knew or ought to have concluded that there was no reasonable prospect that the company would avoid going into insolvent liquidation, and subsequently did not take every step with a view to minimising the potential loss to the company's creditors as he ought to have taken.

The insolvency legislation includes provisions which allow for the adjustment of transactions prior to winding up. This is the case where the company has entered into a "transaction at an undervalue", or has given a "preference" to any of its creditors. The provisions allow for such transactions to be set aside, thus ensuring fairness as between creditors and the beneficiary of any such "transaction at an undervalue".

Under the Company Directors Disqualification Act 1986, directors may be disqualified in a wide variety of circumstances relating to failure to carry out their obligations properly.

(x) Distribution and agency arrangements

An alternative to setting up a subsidiary company or branch of an overseas company in the United Kingdom is to conduct certain business activities, in particular the supply of goods and services, through contractual arrangements, such as distributorship and agency agreements.

Such arrangements and the relationship between the overseas company and its distributor/agent in the United Kingdom and/or Europe are regulated not only by English law but also by EU law.

(a) Distribution agreements

The Treaty of Rome attempts to achieve the removal of private barriers to trade through reliance on the competition provisions of Articles 85 and 86 of the Treaty of Rome. Article 85 prohibits bilateral agreements, conduct or concerted practices between undertakings which prevent, restrict or distort competition and which may affect trade between Member States. Article 86 prevents the abusive exploitation of a dominant position. (See Chapter 12).

There are a number of block exemptions covering standard form agreements which the Commission considers to be pro-competition, and for which it is prepared to give automatic exemption from the provisions of Article 85(1). One of these block exemptions is concerned with exclusive distribution agreements. This block exemption will only apply to agreements between not more than two undertakings for the re-sale of goods, not for services. In return for allocating the distributor an "exclusive" territory (see below) the block exemption allows the principal to include some important restrictions on the activities of the distributor, including:

- an obligation to sell actively only in the territory allotted;
- an obligation not to manufacture or distribute other competing products; and
- an obligation to purchase the contract goods only from the manufacturer.

Including restrictions on competition not expressly authorised by the block exemption will result in the block exemption being unavailable. Clauses which impede the distributor in his free choice of customers, or where either party agrees to refrain from cross border trade cannot therefore be added to the above restrictions. Clauses which infringe the block exemption, and therefore Article 85(1) (and Article 86), are void and unenforceable and potentially submit all parties to fines (see Chapter 12(viii) and (ix) for infringements and enforcement of the rules).

There are essentially three types of distribution agreements:

- *Exclusive distribution agreement*
  An exclusive distribution agreement is one in which the supplier grants distribution rights to a distributor to sell his goods (actively) on an "exclusive" basis within a specified area. The agreements can be drafted to comply with the relevant EU block exemptions (see below). If not, an application for individual exemption and/or negative clearance would have to be made to the Commission.
- *Non-exclusive distribution agreement*
  A non-exclusive distribution agreement is one in which a supplier grants distribution rights to more than one distributor in a given

area. These agreements are not covered by the EU block exemption. Where EU competition rules are applicable the Commission would need to be notified in order to obtain an individual exemption or negative clearance.

- *Selective distribution agreement*
  A selective distribution agreement is one in which the supplier selects a number of distributors to form a network of distributors to sell high quality "specialist" products. The nature of the products concerned generally requires the distributors to employ highly skilled staff. Distributors can be required to sell the product to end users or other network dealers but not to sell to non-members of the network. The selection criteria used to appoint such distributors may only be qualitative not quantative. This means that where a potential distributor meets the manufacturer's objective requirements as to quality of staff and service, he must be accepted into the network. Refusal cannot be made on the basis of the numbers of outlets in a given location.

Practical point

Overseas companies often appoint distributors using standard form agreements or have no written agreement at all. The following should be noted:

- Standard distribution agreements used in most EU countries will often breach EU competition rules;
- Standard distribution agreements often have exclusion clauses restricting liability which are invalid under English law, *i.e.* the result is that there is no limitation on liability;
- Standard form software licence agreements often have clauses preventing copying which are invalid because they breach the EU Copyright Directive (the Directive allows copying for interoperability). The result is that the licence agreement may have no valid restriction on copying at all;
- Overseas judgments, apart from judgment debts, are generally not enforced in the United Kingdom. Therefore the governing law of any

distributorship agreements should be English law to prevent the delays involved in foreign law having to be proved in an English Court;

- In the United Kingdom distribution arrangements are not terminable "at will". Reasonable notice must be given if no notice period is stated in the agreement, or no agreement exists.

(b) "Exclusive" distribution

Where a distributor is given an exclusive sales territory he cannot be given an absolute right or monopoly. "Exclusive" distribution therefore means the right to sell actively within the territory, for example, to seek out customers and promote the product. Responding to or fulfilling "passive" sales, for example, unsolicited calls from purchasers outside the territory cannot be prohibited. In this way, although the manufacturer and distributor benefit from the ability to concentrate sales efforts, national markets are not divided.

Practical point

Many restrictions (*e.g.* non-compete clauses) accepted by two or more parties in the United Kingdom must be registered with the Office of Fair Trading under the Restrictive Trade Practices Act 1976 within three months of the date of the agreement, or the restrictions will be void and therefore unenforceable.

(c) Distinction between agents and distributors

Article 85 applies to arrangements between independent undertakings. However, because of the fundamental difference between the role and powers of a distributor and an agent, the competition rules apply in a very different way to these two types of agreements. A distributor is an undertaking which operates for its own account, fully independent of the manufacturer, buying and selling goods for its own customers. An agent acts as an auxiliary to the manufacturer, selling to the manufacturer's customers on its behalf. Even though the agent may accept certain financial obligations, for example, a *del credere* guarantee, the overall commercial risk is assumed by the manufacturer. Although Article 85 will apply to the agreement between the manufacturer and the distributor, it will not apply to the agency agreement where the agent is merely providing an auxiliary function to the manufacturer's activity of making and selling the goods. In an agency contract it is implicit that the manufacturer can:

- fix the re-sale prices of the goods;
- direct the agents to sell only to certain customers or categories of customers; and
- appoint agents or suppliers for specific territories.

These same obligations would, if contained in a distribution agreement, each amount to a severe restriction on competition.

(d) Agency agreements

Although there are evident benefits for competition law purposes of carrying out distribution through agents, certain obligations may also arise under the national laws of EU member states where an agency arrangement is created, which would not exist where a distribution agreement is used. In particular, since 1 January 1994 new EU rules harmonising terms under which self-employed commercial agents may be appointed have come into force in the United Kingdom. These rules, which have been in force elsewhere in the EU since 1990 (except Eire where they came into force on 1 January 1994), compulsorily write into agency agreements certain provisions.

(e) EU Directive on self-employed commercial agents

A commercial agent for the purposes of the Directive is a self-employed intermediary who has continuing authority to negotiate the sale or the purchase of goods on behalf of another person ("the principal"), or to negotiate and conclude such transactions on behalf of and in the name of phat principal. The Directive does not apply to a distributor who buys and sells or supplies goods on his own account, nor does it apply to agents selling only the services of a principal. Activities on certain commodity markets and exchanges are also excluded although agents of insurance companies and other financial institutions would seem to be within the scope of the Directive if they are self-employed. The Directive does not apply to the supply of services by an agent.

The Directive applies to limited companies as well as self-employed individuals. However, there may not be a commercial agent where:

- promotional material is supplied direct to potential customers; or
- the principal can grant agencies without reference to existing agents; or
- customers normally select the goods themselves and merely place orders through the agent.

The Directive (and UK implementing Regulations) write into any arrangement with an agent (compulsorily) certain terms to protect the agent, including minimum notice periods, defined rights of commission both during and after termination of the arrangements, definitions of duties on each side and confirmation that a non-compete clause can be obtained from the agent. In addition, there is a further right to compensation or an indemnity on termination of the agreement over and above the right to commission after termination. The Directive (and UK implementing Regulations) specify that certain of these rights may not be excluded by contract. In addition, any agreement which does not comply with the Directive (and UK implementing Regulations) or which was concluded before they came into force will be treated as if it does so comply.

(f) Alternative arrangements

In addition to supply of goods through distribution or agency arrangements there are a number of other sales options that might be adopted in the United Kingdom. These include the following:

- the grant of a manufacturing licence to a third party;

- a joint venture with an existing distributor;
- the set-up of an in-house marketing department;
- multi-level marketing; and
- franchising.

3. FOREIGN INVESTMENT

Scope Reasons to invest in the United Kingdom
Financial and other assistance for Businesses starting up in the United Kingdom

(i) Reasons to invest in the United Kingdom

The UK business environment benefits from governmental assistance as outlined below, but, in addition, the following are often cited as reasons to choose the United Kingdom as a base for commencing operations in Europe:

- lowest main corporate tax rate in Europe;
- no exchange controls on profits sent overseas;
- over 80 double taxation treaties with other countries;
- generous capital allowances, including 100% allowances on trade-related research;
- competitive labour costs and the least onerous labour regulations in Europe, with few restrictions on working hours, overtime and holidays, and no legal requirement to recognise a trade union;
- use of English as the "world" language;
- no requirement that shareholders, directors or company secretaries be UK nationals (but see Chapter 7 for the need for overseas nationals to obtain work permits);
- no restrictions on investment by overseas corporations or persons in the United Kingdom;
- group tax relief against losses available when 75% of the group is UK resident;
- deregulation – the UK Government is committed to reducing regulatory and administrative burdens on business;
- an important domestic market, as well as entry to the European market place – the UK domestic market is the third largest in the

European Community, with a population of 58 million and with 22 million households spending more than US $650 million per year on goods and services; UK based companies have access to 370 million consumers in the European Union and are ideally located for contacts with Eastern Europe, the Middle East and British Commonwealth Member States;

- transport and infrastructure – the United Kingdom is the hub of international air travel, has modernised container seaports, and, with the opening of the Channel Tunnel, has improved European links;
- telecommunications – the United Kingdom is the only European country with competitive telecommunications services, with the result that customers get the best and most keenly priced telephone service;
- the UK mailing system is one of the world's most efficient and modern, with postage being among the cheapest rates in the EU;
- resources – the United Kingdom is self-sufficient in energy and has the largest energy resources of any country in the EU; companies setting up in the United Kingdom with requirements over a certain level can negotiate contracts with any regional electricity or generating company in the country, irrespective of their chosen location, which ensures the lowest possible electricity costs and is a benefit not available anywhere else in Europe.

(ii) Financial and other assistance for businesses setting up in the United Kingdom

(a) UK Government assistance

National and local incentives are available to both manufacturing and service companies which invest in the United Kingdom. The UK Government offers regional selective assistance within the assisted areas of England, Wales and Scotland. Grants and other financial help may be available to viable businesses which generate local employment. Incentives for business investment in Northern Ireland are particularly generous.

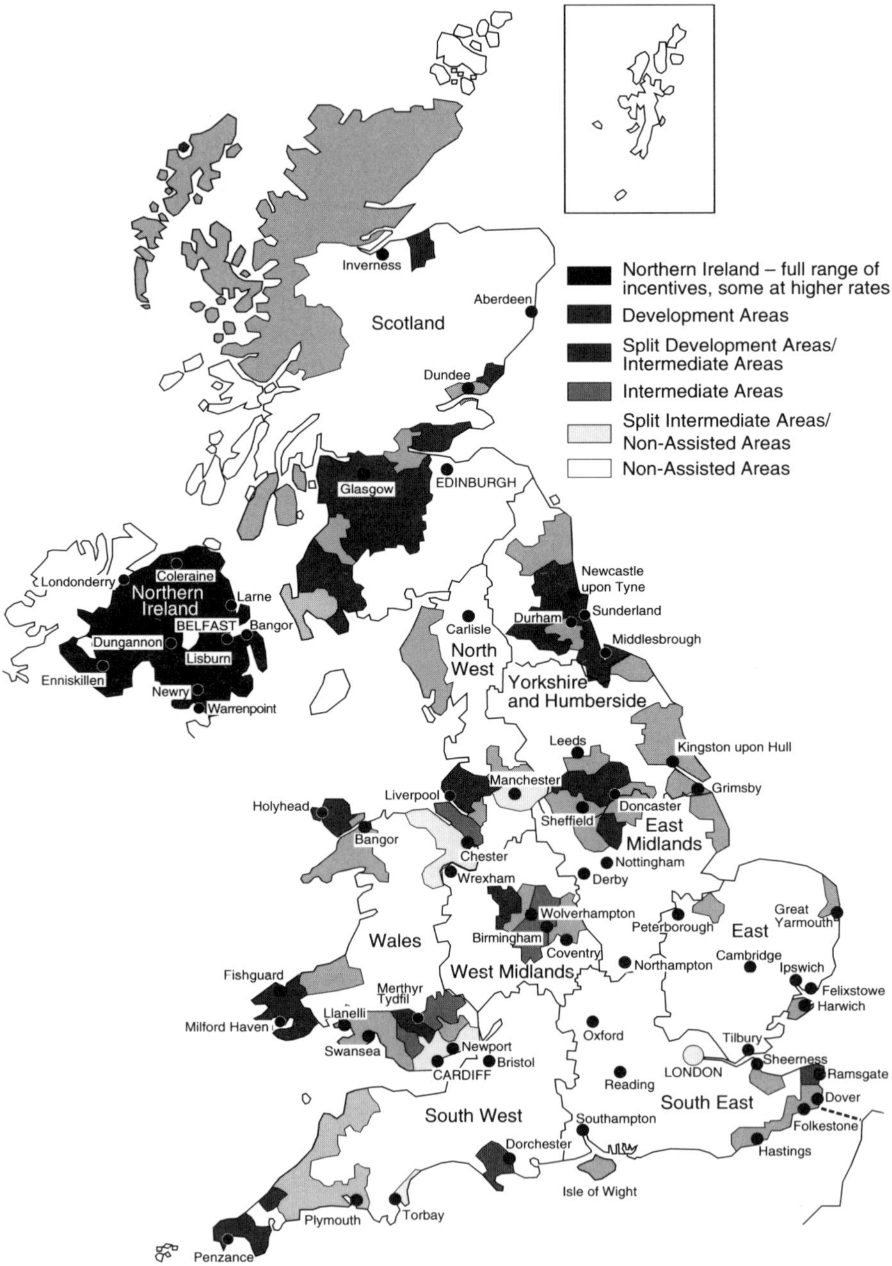

Figure 1. This map was produced with the kind permission of the Invest in Britain Bureau, the UK Government's main inward investment agency, which represents the whole of the UK.

Practical Point

Eligibility for any grants or allowances should be checked with professional advisers or the relevant public body before plans based on the availability of grants or allowances are actioned. Many of the schemes do not allow projects to commence before approval is given.

The incentives to invest in the United Kingdom include the following schemes:

Regional Selective Assistance (RES)

RES is part of the UK Government Department of Trade and Industry's (DTI) Enterprise Initiative Scheme (see below). RES comprises two types of assistance, being Project Grants and Exchange Risk Guarantees.

- *Project grants*
  These form the main type of assistance and are based on the fixed capital costs of a project and the number of jobs expected to be created or safeguarded.
  A company applying for such a grant must show that the project has a good chance of paying its way and that assistance is necessary in order for the company to go ahead with the project on the basis proposed. Further, the project should contribute to both the regional and national economy and create new employment or safeguard existing employment in assisted areas (see map showing UK Assisted areas on p 32).
  No commitment to a project should be given until an offer of assistance is made, since gaining assistance once a project has been commenced is very difficult. Businesses should pursue financing from private sources prior to their application for a grant.
  With certain exceptions, all manufacturing and some service sector projects will qualify for this type of assistance.

- *Exchange risk guarantees*
  The government can offer cover against the exchange risk on low interest foreign currency loans from the European Coal and Steel Community Conversion Loans (see below). Such loans are usually

made in foreign currencies and must be repaid in those currencies. The government covers exchange risk in return for an annual service charge. The scheme is limited to a maximum of £500,000 per project and is targeted at industrial projects. Projects assisted under the scheme should meet the same criteria as for RES (see above).

- *Regional Enterprise Grants*
  Regional Enterprise Grants are available for innovation projects involving the development and introduction of new or improved products or processes. They are available up to a maximum of £25,000 (representing 50% of eligible costs). There is no limit to the size of the project, but there must be some technical risk.
  Additionally a business will only be eligible if it has fewer than 50 employees and sets up in a Development or Intermediate Area (see map showing UK Assisted Areas on p 32).
  A similar scheme is available for investment projects in most manufacturing and some service sectors up to a maximum of £15,000. These, again, are available to businesses setting up in Development Areas but with fewer than 25 employees.
  Regional Selective Assistance Grants are also available to businesses of any size setting up in a Development or Intermediate Area. They are designed to assist projects not eligible under any other scheme and apply to most manufacturing and some service industries. The size of grant is a negotiable matter and will be the minimum necessary. (Historically this has been around 10–15% of eligible capital costs.)

- *Rural Development Commission*
  This is a government body whose aims are to strengthen the rural economy, assisting mainly small businesses in "priority areas". It is organised on a regional basis, offering not only financial assistance, but information and expertise as well.

DTI and other government initiatives

Further information can be obtained from the persons specified below:

- Invest in Britain Bureau
  Department of Trade and Industry
  Kingsgate House
  66–74 Victoria Street

London SW1E 6SW
0171-215-2501

- Enterprise Zones
  Contact : (DoE) 0171-276-6166
- Inner Cities
  City Grant
  Contact : (English Partnership) 0171-976-3216
  Urban Programme
  Contact : (DoE) 0171-276-4491
- Regional Enterprise Grants
  Contact : (DTI) 0171-215-8460
- European Loans and Exchange Risk Cover
  Contact : (DTI) 0171-215-2604
- Loan Guarantee Scheme
  Contact : (DTI) 01742-701356 (ext 7312)
- Business Expansion Scheme
  Contact : 0171-438-6720
- Derelict Land Grant
  Contact : (English Partnership) 0171-976-3204
- Enterprise Allowance Scheme
  Contact : Local Job Centre
- Training and Enterprise Councils (TECs)
  Contact : Local Job Centre

(b) EU loans and grants

EU assistance and investment incentives include the following:

- *European Investment Bank loans (EIB)*
  The EIB provides loans for capital investment projects in industry and related services mainly in the EU assisted areas. The size of the loan normally begins at about £7,000,000 (being a maximum of half the project's cost) but smaller loans for medium-sized companies are available. Loans from the EIB provide one of the few

funds where eligibility is not conditional on the nationality of, or legal status of, the borrower, although projects must normally be carried out within the territories of Member States (although even this can be waived with permission of the Board of Governors).

- *European Coal and Steel Community conversion loans (ECSC)*
  The ECSC provides fixed interest rate medium-term loans for projects creating new jobs in areas that have suffered job losses in the coal and steel industries. Loans are for up to half the fixed asset costs of the project.

- *European Regional Development Fund (ERDF)*
  The aim of the ERDF is to help correct regional imbalances within the European Union. An allocation of funds between the Member States is made on a quota basis. Areas and regions are established by Member States for the application of national regional aid, and it is these areas to which fund aid may be directed. Approximately two thirds of grants made are for infrastructure projects which are undertaken by local authorities or other public bodies and are intended to reduce the amount such bodies may have to borrow to finance investments. It is usual for the fund to provide approximately 50% of the total public expenditure. Examples of specific infrastructure projects which have been assisted include the construction of the dam and connecting aqueducts at Kielder for the Northumbrian Water Authority, the resignalling and modernisation of South Yorkshire's railways for British Rail, and the provision of gas storage facilities in South East Wales for British Gas.

  Grants are also available from the ERDF to individual companies in the industry and service sector. The fund may contribute in respect of such investments in industrial or service activities up to 20% of the investment cost, provided that such contribution does not exceed 50% of the aid accorded by public authorities in regional aids. The contributions are further limited to that part of the investment which does not exceed a specified ECU amount per job created, and a further ECU amount per job maintained. State aids to be taken into consideration are grants, interest rebates or their equivalent, where loans at reduced rates of interest are concerned, and also whether such aid is linked to the investment or to the number of jobs created. Certain other aid equivalents may be taken into account such as rent rebates or exemptions from payment of rent for buildings. In the United Kingdom investors do not receive additional assistance as a result of being awarded an ERDF grant as the government uses it as partial repayment of existing government aid.

- *European Social Fund (ESF)*
  The ESF provides funding to organisations running schemes for vocational training and job creation. Public authorities must provide at least as much funding as that sought from the ESF. Individual companies can apply, but they must obtain some funding from a public authority to be eligible for a grant.

- *EU Research and Development Programme*
  A fourth Research and Development programme covering the period 1994 to 1998 is currently in operation, with the European Commission continuing the process of identifying specific projects and then identifying and selecting contractors to carry out those projects. Funds are being allocated for research and development projects in the following general areas: information and communications technologies; industrial and materials technologies; biotechnology; the environment; energy; and human capacity and the mobility of the workforce.

- *Eureka*
  Eureka encourages industry-led European collaborative projects aimed at producing hi-tech goods and services to compete successfully worldwide. It covers the entire range of research and development in high technology and provides a "matchmaking" service to bring products and partners together. Eureka participants can request support from their governments in removing market barriers, for example, through harmonising standards to open up the European market.

4. FINANCING UK OPERATIONS

Scope

Debt financing
Start up capital
Venture capital
Development capital
Raising money on the London Stock Exchange
Overseas companies listing on the London Stock Exchange
Alternative Investment Market (AIM)
The Panel on Takeovers and Mergers

(i) Debt financing

(a) Short term finance

Short term finance is usually provided by way of bank overdraft. Overdrafts can deal with problems of cash flow, take advantage of changing market conditions, and generally finance working capital. The terms of an overdraft are usually evidenced by a letter which states that the overdraft is repayable on demand by the bank.

(b) Medium term finance

Medium term finance is usually provided by way of bank term loan with standard conditions applying, which often include a repayment schedule and conditions as to the use of the funds. Such a loan is not usually repayable on demand but rather on the occurrence of certain events connected with the solvency of the borrower and the running of the loan facility. Security is normally required by a lender where available.

(c) Long term finance

Long term commercial loans are not usually popular with UK banks.

If the funding requirement is for longer than seven years then the bank usually will look for this to be funded by a share investment.

(d) UK lending formalities

Loans from a bank or other financial institution may be syndicated, depending on the size of the loan and the required spreading of risk. Banks and other financial institutions will usually insist on formal documentation in respect of medium and long term loans. Loan agreements will include provisions for the following:

- *Interest*
  This differs according to the purpose of the loan and the status of the borrower, and on shorter term loans is geared to the particular bank's base lending rate. On medium term loans, interest is normally linked to the floating London Inter Bank Offered Rate (LIBOR), which is charged on the outstanding balance of the loan. Sometimes interest is fixed at the time the loan is taken up. The extent of any security provided is reflected in the interest rate charged.
- *Other costs and fees*
  An arrangement fee may be charged by the relevant lending institution in setting up the facility. A pre-payment fee will often be charged on the early repayment of the loan and a non-utilisation fee where the full amount of the loan made available by a bank has not been utilised by the borrower.
- *Security*
  This will be taken by a bank, where available, whether by a charge (a security interest) over the borrower's property and assets, or in the form of guarantees from group companies or directors. Security provided will depend on the bargaining position of the borrower and may be limited to a particular project for which the finance is being provided and may not be required over the business as a whole.

  The most usual form of secured borrowing is by a **debenture**, with the security being provided by way of a **fixed and floating charge**. In general a fixed charge is given over real property and ensures the property charged cannot be dealt with except subject to the lender's interest. A floating charge allows more flexibility as the borrower can continue to deal with its assets. A floating charge will often be required by a lender to the extent that it enables the lender to appoint its own receiver on the insolvency of the company and deal with the assets secured to its own advantage. Charging documents will usually contain restrictions preventing the borrower from creating subsequent security without the lender's consent, and if such consent is given banks will usually wish to complete a priority agreement regulating their respective security rights. Loans from other sources, especially from non-institutional lenders, are often subordinated to the principal debt. Charges must be registered with the Registrar of Companies within 21 days of their creation in order to be enforceable against the borrower.

(ii) Start up capital

The principal source of start up capital for a business tends to be from the proprietor of the business (and his or her associates). Other sources include:

- loan finance, usually provided by a clearing bank by way of overdraft or possibly a term loan. Such loan facilities usually require a personal guarantee or some other form of collateral security by the proprietor;
- a number of specialised institutions (in both public and private sectors) who provide support by way of loans or subscriptions for shares, or a mixture of the two. None of these, however, exist specifically to help new businesses and, on the whole, the funds available from these sources are limited;
- business proprietors with established connections may be able to obtain indirect finance in the form of trade credit from suppliers with an interest in fostering the development of the business;
- leasing is especially useful for companies not anticipating incurring immediate tax liabilities and thereby being unable to obtain the maximum benefits from tax allowances available in respect of capital expenditure; and
- hire purchase is another alternative, but does not possess the tax advantages of leasing. It may nevertheless reduce a company's immediate financing requirements and release funds which would otherwise be tied up.

(iii) Venture capital

In the United Kingdom there is a mature and competitive venture capital industry. The largest venture capital company is 3i plc, but it has over 100 competitors.

Venture capitalists look to invest in a company with a good product, a market where the company can attain a protected position, high margins, and most importantly a management team with direct experience of the product and its market. The management team must demonstrate a strong commitment to the project, in addition to self-confidence and a real ambition to turn their business plan into reality.

Those prepared to invest in higher risk ventures understandably seek to minimise the risk involved and, in so doing, demand both the means of capitalising on the success of the venture (which in practice usually means taking a stake in the equity) and obtaining the best possible safeguards in case the venture turns out badly.

The form and availability of financing from a venture capitalist depends on the degree of risk and the prospect of future profits.

Practical point

The British Venture Capital Association represents the major sources of venture capital in the United Kingdom. It publishes useful guides and directories. (To find out more about the Association telephone 0171 240 3846 or Fax 0171 240 3849.)

(iv) Development capital

The methods of financing development capital differ considerably among the various sectors of industry and commerce. Many enterprises rely heavily on bank facilities, both temporary and long term loans.

Small and medium size companies do not have access to the capital markets, which are largely controlled by the London Stock Exchange. The costs and obligations associated with the obtaining of a full Stock Exchange listing are high. However, there is now a gateway procedure for companies listed elsewhere in the EU to obtain a listing in London which costs a fraction of traditional methods. Securities which are not listed have certain tax advantages over listed securities.

Finance for development capital may also be available from government sources by way of assistance from the Department of Trade and Industry or through a government agency (see Chapter 3).

Indirect financing is also important to established businesses. This includes:

- trade credit;
- leasing arrangements;
- hire purchase and credit factoring (more often used by small or medium size companies);
- bills of exchange (restricted to larger companies possessing the necessary financial standing).

(v) Raising money on the London Stock Exchange

The London Stock Exchange is authorised under the Financial Services Act 1986 to make listing rules (commonly known as the Yellow Book). If a company applies for listing it must comply with the listing rules before its securities will be admitted to the Official List of the London Stock Exchange.

(a) Sponsors

A company seeking to list its securities must have a sponsor:

- when listing particulars are being produced;
- when the Exchange requires a sponsor after a breach of the listing rules;
- when a sponsor is required by the listing rules to report to the Exchange in relation to a transaction.

At other times, while the Exchange may encourage the appointment of a sponsor to give advice on a continuing basis, it does not require one to be appointed. The requirements for being a sponsor are that the sponsor must:

- be an authorised person under the Financial Services Act 1986;
- satisfy the Exchange that it is competent to discharge the responsibilities of a sponsor;
- give a signed undertaking to the Exchange; and
- be on the Exchange's Register of Sponsors.

The responsibilities of a sponsor include:

- satisfying itself that the issuer has satisfied all relevant conditions for listing;
- ensuring that the issuer is guided and advised as to the application of listing rules;
- being satisfied that the directors have had explained to them the nature of their responsibilities and their obligations as directors of a listed company;
- reporting that it has written confirmation that the directors have established procedures for them to make proper judgments as to the financial position and prospects of the company;
- in the case of a new applicant, reporting on whether an accountant's report is required;
- in connection with the working capital statement, reporting that it has written confirmation that the capital available to the group is sufficient for its requirements;
- where there is a profit forecast, reporting that it is satisfied that the profit forecast has been made after due and careful enquiry.

Practical point

The London Stock Exchange requires every applicant to the Official List to have a sponsor. A sponsor's role in the procedure is to act as the formal link between the company and the Exchange and to assist the company to comply with the listing rules and to present its case to the Exchange. For companies already listed elsewhere in the EU the procedure is heavily biased towards the legal work. It therefore makes sense for the lawyer (provided he has the experience and contacts within the Exchange) to offer a dual service of acting both as sponsor and solicitor.

(b) Conditions for listing

An applicant for listing must have three years' audited accounts. The auditors' report must be unqualified (regarding any matter of significance for investors). There are exceptions to this three year rule, such as when dealing with a major capital project.

An applicant for listing must also have been carrying on as its main activity an independent business which is revenue earning for a three year period. There must have been continuity of management throughout the three year period. In assessing this the Exchange considers whether:

- the current executive directors have had, collectively, direct management responsibility for all the group's major businesses;
- the current key executive directors have played a significant role in the group's activities;
- the senior management taken as a whole has changed materially.

An applicant must ensure that each of its directors is free of conflict between duty to the company and private interests. Where there is a controlling shareholder (defined as one which has 30% or more of the votes), the company must be capable of operating and making decisions independent of that shareholder. All transactions and relationships in the future between the company and the controlling shareholder must be at arm's length and on a normal commercial basis. All significant decisions by the directors must be taken by a majority who are independent of the controlling shareholder.

The expected market value of securities to be listed must be at least £700,000 for shares and £200,000 for debt.

At least 25% of a class of shares to be listed must be in the hands of the public. Shares will not be regarded as being held in public hands if they are held by:

- a director;
- a person connected with a director;
- the trustees of any employees' share scheme or pension fund established for directors and employees;
- any person who has the right to nominate a director; or
- any person who is interested in 5% or more of the shares of the

relevant class (unless the Exchange otherwise determines that such a person can be included).

(c) Methods of bringing securities to listing

The methods available depend on whether or not equity shares are already listed. An applicant without equity shares already listed, seeking to list shares worth less than £25,000,000 may list shares by means of:

- introduction – only available when the shares are already widely held by the public;
- offer for sale – an invitation to the public on behalf of a third party in respect of shares already in issue;
- offer for subscription – an invitation to the public by the company to subscribe for shares not yet in issue;
- placing – a marketing of securities to specified persons or clients of a sponsor; or
- intermediaries' offer – a marketing of securities by the issuer to intermediaries for them to allocate to their own clients.

(d) Listing particulars

The **listing rules** contain details of what must be disclosed in listing particulars.

In addition, there is a **general duty of disclosure** contained in section 146 of the Financial Services Act 1986. This requires listing particulars to contain all such information as investors and their professional advisers would reasonably require, and reasonably expect to find there, for the purpose of making an informed assessment of:

- the assets and liabilities, financial position, profits and losses and prospects of the issuer of the securities; and
- the rights attaching to those securities.

Section 152 of the Financial Services Act 1986 states that the person responsible for listing particulars includes not only the issuer for securities but each director.

(e) Continuing obligations

A company has general obligations of disclosure as well as specific obligations of disclosure.

A company must notify the Exchange without delay of any major new developments in its sphere of activity which are not public knowledge and which may, by virtue of the effect of those developments on its assets and liabilities, financial position, or general course of its business, lead to substantial movement in the price of its listed securities.

Where to the knowledge of the company's directors there is such a change in the company's financial condition or in the performance of its business or in the company's expectation of its performance that knowledge of the change is likely to lead to substantial movement in the price of its listed securities, the company must notify to the Exchange without delay all relevant information concerning the change. The notification must include sufficient information concerning the change as, together with other information that it has previously made available in accordance with the listing rules, will enable the value of its listed securities to be determined.

A company need not notify the Exchange of impending developments or matters in the course of negotiation.

(f) Classification of transactions

The listing rules classify transactions by assessing the size of the transaction relative to the size of the listed company. The classification is made by looking at the percentage ratios of such matters as assets to assets and profits to profits of the company and the target respectively. The transaction is then classified as Class 3 (less than 5%), Class 2 (5–15%), Class 1 (15–25%), Super Class 1 (25% +) or Reverse Takeover (100% +). Depending on the classification, the company will have to make a public announcement, send an explanatory circular to shareholders, obtain prior approval of shareholders or issue listing particulars.

(g) Transactions with related parties

A related party means a substantial shareholder (entitled to exercise 10% or more of the votes), an associate of a substantial shareholder, a director or an associate of a director. An associate includes an individual's spouse or child and trustees where an individual or an individual's family is a beneficiary under the trust.

The usual requirements for a transaction with a related party is that the listed company must:

- make an announcement through the Exchange;
- send a circular to its shareholders;
- obtain the approval of the shareholders; and
- ensure that the related party abstains from voting on the relevant resolution.

There are exceptions to the usual requirements, including an exception for small transactions. There are no rules applying where all of the percentage ratios for classification purposes are less than 0.25%. Where the percentage ratios are between 0.25% and less than 5%, the usual requirements do not apply, and instead the company must:

- inform the Exchange of the proposed transaction;
- provide the Exchange with confirmation from an independent adviser that the terms of the proposed transaction with a related party are fair and reasonable so far as the shareholders of the company are concerned; and
- include details of the transaction in the company's next published annual accounts.

(h) Directors

Every three years a listed company must submit a declaration by each of its directors as to their business activities. This is submitted to the Securities and Futures Authority.

A declaration must also be submitted on the appointment of a new director or when any important change in the functions or executive responsibilities of a director occurs.

Copies of all the directors' service contracts must be made available for inspection at the registered office of the company from the date of the notice convening the company's annual general meeting (AGM) up to the close of that meeting, and at the place of the AGM for at least fifteen minutes prior to and during that meeting. Each director's service contract available for inspection must disclose or have attached to it any matters necessary to enable investors to estimate the possible liability of the company upon early termination of the contract.

A company must notify the Exchange of any information which is disclosed to the company in accordance with section 324 of the Companies Act 1985. This relates to the duty of a director to disclose shareholdings in his own company. The provisions also extend to dealings by spouses, children, certain trustees and partners of the directors. Details of any options held by directors must also be disclosed.

(i) Mineral companies

A mineral company is a company whose principal activity is the extraction of mineral resources. A mineral company may be listed on the Exchange without a three year track record of audited accounts or three years of independent business which is revenue earning and under continuous management. The main difference in relation to the listing particulars is that a competent person's report must be included. This report must inform prospective investors about such matters as the mineral reserves, long term prospects, forecast extraction rates and valuation of mineral reserves.

(j) Scientific research based companies

Scientific research based companies are companies which are primarily involved in the laboratory research and development of chemical or biological products or processes and may include, subject to the agreement of the Exchange, other similar innovative science-based companies. The main points include the company:

- does not require three years as an independent revenue earning business;
- the applicant must have already attracted funds from "sophisticated investors";
- the applicant must be raising at least £10m and have a capitalisation of at least £20m; and

- the applicant must demonstrate to the satisfaction of the Exchange that it has achieved significant commercial milestones in its development as a scientific research based company.

Directors, major shareholders and senior employees may not dispose of shares for two years following listing. The exception to this rule is that major shareholders may dispose of up to 40% of their holdings after the publication of the first financial results of the company following listing (with a minimum holding period of six months). Any application which appears to be primarily intended to enable the sale of shares of existing shareholders will be rejected.

The listing particulars of a scientific research based company must include an independent report on the merits of the company's products.

(vi) Overseas companies listing on the London Stock Exchange

(a) Primary or secondary listing

Chapter 17 of the listing rules of the London Stock Exchange contains modifications to the listing rules in respect of overseas companies. Most of the modifications to the rules depend on whether the overseas company is seeking a primary or secondary listing in the United Kingdom. The primary listing will often be in the country of incorporation.

(b) SEAQ International

Securities are eligible for trading on SEAQ International if they are listed, quoted or dealt, on any stock exchange **approved by** the London Stock Exchange. SEAQ International gives access to the major institutional investors and means that the company does not have to comply with the detailed provisions of the listing rules.

However, SEAQ International does not have the public visibility of a listing in London. It is only by a listing on the London Stock Exchange that a company enters into a continuing direct relationship with the Exchange whereby the company provides information to the market place through the Exchange's news service. Such information supports trading in a company's shares, by improving both the awareness and understanding of the company by investors and market intermediaries.

(c) Listing rules relating to a secondary listing

An overseas company seeking a secondary listing on the London Stock Exchange must take into account the following:

- Accounts – if the Exchange is satisfied that an overseas company's accounts have been prepared to a standard appropriate for a company of international standing and repute, it may accept standards different from the normal UK standards. However, the overseas company should consult the Exchange at an early stage regarding its accounts.
- Existing documents – the overseas company may incorporate in its listing particulars relevant documents which have been published in accordance with the rules of its primary regulator.
- Sponsor – an overseas company, like a UK company, will need a sponsor for its application for listing.
- Conditions for listing – these conditions include the Exchange being satisfied that the overseas applicant has complied with the requirements of its primary regulator.
- Continuing obligations – the usual continuing obligations do not apply to overseas companies seeking a secondary listing; however, special continuing obligations also apply. These include obligations to notify changes in directors and changes in interests of major shareholders. There are obligations also in relation to communication with shareholders, such as distributing circulars, giving information on payment of dividends and the issue of new securities. There are also rules relating to annual accounts having to be independently audited.
- Mutual recognition – a document issued by an overseas company and approved by a competent authority of another EU member state will qualify as listing particulars, providing certain conditions are satisfied. These mutual recognition provisions do not extend beyond the EU.
- EU listed companies – a company already listed for not less than three years in another member state of the EU is eligible for the

gateway procedure for a full listing on the London Stock Exchange. To use the new simplified procedure there must be no simultaneous marketing (*i.e.* public offering) of further securities. The listing document for this procedure must be published within 42 days of the date on which the auditors sign their report on the accounts of the company.

(vii) **Alternative Investment Market (AIM)**

The London Stock Exchange has introduced the Alternative Investment Market (AIM) for young, growing companies. A company seeking admission to AIM must comply with the Rules of the London Stock Exchange and also publish a prospectus. The prospectus must comply with the Public Offers of Securities (POS) Regulations, due to be enacted in April 1995. AIM requirements are different from the Official List requirements in a number of ways, such as no need for a sponsor and no minimum shareholding by the public. However, AIM companies have similar obligations to Official List companies to disclose information to the Exchange.

(viii) **The Panel on Takeovers and Mergers**

Following widespread criticism of certain take-over practices, the Panel on Takeovers and Mergers was established in 1968. The Panel publishes the City Code on Takeovers and Mergers, and the Rules Governing Substantial Acquisitions of Shares.

The Code and the Panel operate principally to ensure fair and equal treatment of all shareholders in relation to takeovers. The Code provides an orderly framework within which takeovers are conducted, but is not concerned with the financial or commercial advantages or disadvantages of a takeover.

The Code applies to public companies (whether listed or unlisted), to those persons seeking to takeover a public company, to directors and to professional advisers.

In takeovers and mergers care should also be taken to ensure compliance with the provisions of the Fair Trading Act and the provisions of the EU Merger Regulation (see Chapter 12).

5. SUPPLY OF GOODS AND SERVICES

Scope

Implied Terms
Consumer credit
Consumer protection
Labelling
Weights and Measures
Advertising and promotions
Data Protection
Technical harmonisation and standards

(i) Implied terms

The supply of goods or the provision of services in the United Kingdom is regulated by a very considerable amount of legislation and regulation. Under the Sale of Goods Act 1979, as amended by the Sale and Supply of Goods Act 1994, certain fundamental terms are implied into every contract for the sale of goods. These are:

- that the seller has good title to the goods concerned;
- that the goods will be of satisfactory quality;
- that where the buyer has made a specific purpose known the goods will be reasonably fit for the purpose (even if it is not the purpose for which the goods are commonly supplied);
- that in the case of a sale by description or sample, the goods actually sold will correspond to the description or sample.

In the case of the provision of services in the course of the supplier's business, there are implied terms that the services concerned will be supplied at a reasonable cost, within a reasonable time, and provided with reasonable care and skill.

Hiring agreements may also include terms implied by the Supply of Goods and Services Act 1982 and may in certain circumstances be regulated agreements under the Consumer Credit Act 1974 (see below).

(ii) Consumer credit

The giving of credit in the United Kingdom is closely regulated where the credit transaction falls within the Consumer Credit Act 1974. This will be the case where:

- the debtor is an "individual", *i.e.* not a company (although sole proprietors and partnerships are included);
- the amount of credit involved does not exceed £15,000; and
- the agreement extends for a period in excess of three months.

If regulated under the Act, then the company giving the credit must be registered under the Act before entering any agreements, otherwise:

- the company and the directors will commit a criminal offence; and
- the agreement will be unenforceable by the company (but will still be enforceable by the debtor).

If an agreement is regulated, it may in certain circumstances be subject to rights of cancellation, and will require special notice to be given to the debtor before the relevant obligations can be enforced. In addition, the agreement must contain certain information and statements in a prescribed form. If any of the rules set out in the Act are not followed, the agreement will be improperly executed and may be unenforceable.

(iii) Consumer protection

The United Kingdom implemented the EU Product Liability Directive in the form of the Consumer Protection Act 1987. The Act makes producers ("producers") liable for defects in products to consumers. Producers for the purpose of the Act include:

- manufacturers of finished products or component parts or producers of any raw materials;

- any person who by his trade mark presents himself as the producer, *i.e.* own branders;
- importers into the EU (unless the overseas manufacturer can be identified).

Liability arises in respect of defects in all moveable products except agricultural products and game. A product is defective if it does not provide the safety which a person is entitled to expect taking all circumstances into account, for example, the presentation of the product and its reasonably expected use at the time it was put into circulation. A producer will be liable for death or personal injury and damage to property. It should be noted that the United Kingdom has not imposed a financial limit on the total amount of damages payable in respect of liability under the Act, whereas a number of other European States have set monetary limits.

There are a number of defences available, including the following:

- that the defect was due to compliance with the mandatory regulations of a public authority;
- that the state of scientific and technical knowledge at the time when the product was put into circulation was not such as to enable the existence of the defect to be discovered, *i.e.* the state of the art defence; and
- that the defect is attributable to the design of the product of which the component is a part, or following instructions given by the manufacturer of the product of which the component is a part.

It is not possible to exclude liability under the Act by contract. Any attempt to do so will be void and unenforceable.

(iv) **Labelling**

There are specific regulations which set out the requirements for labelling of certain products. Areas which are particularly highly regulated include food, pharmaceuticals, cosmetics, hazardous substances, tobacco products, electrical appliances, textiles, etc. In addition, it should be noted that in the case of pharmaceuticals, all medicinal products are required to be licensed by the Department of Health prior to import, manufacture and/or sale in the United Kingdom.

The Trade Descriptions Act 1968 makes it a criminal offence in the course of a trade or business to apply a false trade description to any goods, or to supply or offer to supply any goods to which a false trade description is applied.

(v) Weights and measures

There are complex and detailed regulations concerning weights and measures for goods and marking of the same on packaging and labelling. Note that indications of weights and measures are deemed to be trade descriptions for the purpose of the Trade Descriptions Act 1968 (see above).

(vi) Advertising and promotions

Advertising and promotions are regulated in the United Kingdom under statute by the Misleading Advertisements Regulations 1988, and by industry self-regulation under the Advertising Standards Authority Code of Practice and the British Code of Sales Promotion Practice. In addition, there are various other voluntary codes of practice which relate to particular industries such as the pharmaceutical industry and mail order publishers. These codes all establish standards and conduct with which the members of the issuing associations or organisations agree to comply.

Where the provisions of any such codes are contravened there is generally a complaints procedure, but usually the threat of adverse publicity is sufficient to secure adherence to the codes. The legal concepts of character merchandising, passing off, and trade mark and copyright protection also apply.

(vii) Data protection

Under the Data Protection Act 1984 where a person or organisation controls the contents and use of a collection of **personal data** (*i.e.* relating to living individuals, known as "data subjects") which is processed automatically, such person or organisation is a **data user** and is required to register under the Act, unless the personal data falls within one of the exemptions specified in the Act. Once effected, registration is valid for three years unless the data user opts for a lesser period. The Act gives data subjects a right of access to the personal data held, a right of compensation for damage because of an inaccuracy in the data held, and a right to complain to the Data Protection Registrar or to apply to the courts for correction or deletion of inaccurate data.

Practical Point

The Act applies to all data users who control and use personal data in the United Kingdom. If a non-UK resident holding company exercises control of personal data through its UK subsidiary then it is the UK subsidiary company which should register as the data user. Only if the non-UK resident holding company directly controls and uses the processed data in the United Kingdom (*i.e.* independently of its UK subsidiary) will it need to be registered a data user.

(viii) Technical harmonisation and standards

In common with the other member states of the European Union, the United Kingdom imposes obligations on manufacturers and suppliers in the interests of safety and consumer protection.

Gradually European legislation (in the form of Directives) has been introduced, with the aim of ensuring a harmonised approach to safety/consumer protection issues and to removing the barriers to trade that are caused by national laws.

The various European Directives set down "attestation" procedures by which one can assess whether a product complies with what is known as the "essential safety requirements". Products to which the Directives apply must go through the attestation procedures before being offered for sale in the United Kingdom or elsewhere in the European Union.

In cases involving high risk products, assessment for conformity must be carried out by an approved independent testing house.

Products conforming with the Directive requirements will, in most cases, be required to be marked with what is known as the "CE" mark. This mark is therefore a symbol of conformity with particular standards. Currently it is applied to such diverse products as toys, gas appliances, medical devices, personal protective equipment, telecommunications terminal equipment, and construction products.

It is an offence to apply the "CE" mark to goods which do not conform to the relevant standards.

6. EMPLOYMENT (LABOUR LAW)

Scope

Terms of employment
Discrimination
Employment security
Maternity rights
Health and safety at work
Liability/insurance
Other employment rights
Transfer of business
Pensions
Strikes
EU employment issues

(i) Terms of employment

Whether an employment contract is written or oral, an employer must, not later than two months after the employee starts work, give the employee a written statement containing certain particulars. The statement must identify the contracting parties and specify the date when the employment began and the date when the employee's period of continuous employment began (usually the same date). The period of continuous employment is used for calculating (amongst other things) redundancy pay when this is applicable. The statement must also contain details regarding the following:

- the rate of pay and how it is calculated;
- the intervals of payment;
- the terms and conditions relating to hours of work;
- holidays and holiday pay;
- sickness or injury provisions and sick pay;
- pension schemes, and whether or not a contracting out certificate has been issued (or a statement that there is no such scheme);
- the notice necessary to end the contract (or the date the contract expires if for a fixed term);

- the employee's job title;
- the employee's place of work;
- the disciplinary rules and procedures;
- the grievance procedures; and
- the details of any collective agreements directly affecting the terms of employment;
- if an employee is required to work outside the United Kingdom for a period for more than one month, details of the terms that will apply to the period of time spent abroad.

If any of the provisions are contained in another document, the statement may refer the employee to such document, although the rate of pay; the intervals of payment; the terms and conditions relating to hours of work; holidays and holiday pay; the employee's job title; and the employee's place of work must always be included in a single document.

There must be no change in the contractual terms without the employee's consent and if there is an agreed change in a contractual term, written particulars must be sent to the employee within a month of the change.

Practical Point

If an employer is changing an employee's contract for the worse (*e.g.* introducing a new restrictive covenant) the best time to deal with it is when he is also changing it for the better (*e.g.* at the time of a pay increase). This is however a complex area involving the law of constructive dismissal and legal advice must be sought.

In addition to a written statement of the terms and conditions of employment it is usual for the employee to be informed that some or all of the information which he will be given concerning the company's business and future activities is confidential and must be kept confidential by him. (This is discussed further in Chapter 8(x) below). Where the employee is engaged in research and development work it is important to include a clause whereby the results of the employee's work are owned by the company. (See Chapter 8 for a further discussion on this point).

Practical Point

Confidentiality and proprietary information agreements drafted to comply with an overseas company's foreign law need to be redrafted to comply with English law as they tend to be either inappropriate or ineffective.

A further option when preparing a statement of terms and conditions, is to include a form of restrictive covenant. These clauses are sometimes also referred to as non-compete clauses, and seek to prevent the employee from damaging his or her employer's business after the employee has left, by using the employer's name or contacts which the employee has made during the course of his employment (with clients or employees of the employer) to conduct a similar form of business in competition with the employer. As a matter of public policy, courts will only uphold such clauses to the extent that they are reasonably required for the protection of the employer's legitimate interests.

Practical Point

It is possible to have a valid non-compete clause for key personnel. This can prevent, for instance, key salesmen moving to a direct competitor for a defined period time after termination of his employment. The law on these clauses is continually changing and legal advice should be sought when any clause is being drafted.

(ii) Discrimination

There are a number of provisions dealing with the question of discrimination in employment. Under both UK and EU law there is a right to equal pay for people doing work of equal value. The work should be the same or of a broadly similar nature and should involve a similar degree of responsibility. The Equal Pay Act 1970 implies an "equality clause" into every contract of employment. This will operate to modify contractual terms where a member of one sex is employed under a contract which contains terms less beneficial than those enjoyed by an employee of the opposite sex doing comparable work. Discrimination on the grounds of sex or marital status is unlawful. Likewise discrimination on racial grounds, that is grounds of colour, race, nationality or ethnic or national origins is also unlawful.

"Discrimination" includes direct discrimination where one employee is treated less favourably than another on the grounds of race or sex. Also covered are indirect discrimination and discrimination by victimisation. The former covers situations where the requirements imposed upon people of different sex or race are identical, but:

- the very nature of them means that far fewer people of a certain race/sex can comply with them;
- this cannot be shown to be justified; and
- it is to the detriment of the person who cannot comply.

Discrimination by victimisation concerns the situation where an employee is treated less favourably because he has taken action under the anti-discrimination legislation against perceived discrimination.

Where a claim of sexual or racial discrimination is successfully made in an industrial tribunal there are no limits on the compensation which the tribunal may award.

(iii) Employment security

Unfair dismissal

After a period of two years' continuous employment, an employee has a right not be unfairly dismissed. If an employer dismisses such an employee without good reason, or without following a fair procedure, this may constitute unfair dismissal. Dismissal will potentially be fair if:

- relating to the capability/qualifications of the employee for doing that particular kind of work;
- relating to the employee's conduct;
- the employee was being made redundant;
- continuing employment would contravene an enactment; or
- there is some other substantial reason justifying it.

In all the above circumstances, the employer must also be able to show that it acted reasonably in treating that reason as sufficient for dismissing the employee.

Issues relating to the dismissal of employees are decided by an Industrial Tribunal, the members of which are comprised of representatives of employers' and employees' bodies as well as a legally qualified chairman. The Tribunal has a discretion as to which of the following remedies it prescribes if it finds there was indeed an unfair dismissal.

- **Reinstatement** – the employee is reinstated to the job which he or she held prior to the dismissal and must be treated as if there was no dismissal.
- **Re-engagement** – the employee is re-engaged in employment comparable to that from which he or she was dismissed or in other suitable employment.
- **Compensation** – this consists of a basic award and a compensatory award. The basic award is calculated using a formula based on basic weekly pay, length of service, and age, and is subject to a maximum week's pay of £205. The compensatory award, which has a maximum of £11,000, is calculated by assessing the employee's actual loss and then taking into account any payments already made to the employee.

Compensation may be awarded in addition to an order for reinstatement or re-engagement.

Redundancy

Employees who lose their jobs in certain circumstances have a right to receive a redundancy payment. There are detailed provisions relating to redundancy but broadly speaking an employee is entitled to redundancy payment if he or she has been continuously employed for at least two years at the date the contract ends and is dismissed by reason of redundancy. This covers a situation where:

- the employer ceased to carry on the business for which the employee was employed, or ceased to carry it on in the place where the employee was employed; or
- the requirements of that business for employees doing work of that particular kind in that place have ceased or diminished or are expected to cease or diminish.

An employer must notify any recognised trade union (*i.e.* a union recognised by the employer for the purpose of collective bargaining) of any forthcoming redundancies and must also notify the Secretary of State for Employment if the redundancies involve ten or more employees.

The provisions relating to unfair dismissal and redundancy now also relate to part-time employees.

(iv) **Maternity rights**

A pregnant employee has the following statutory rights:

- not to be unreasonably refused time off during her working hours to receive ante-natal care and to be paid for the time of her absence at the appropriate rate;
- not to be dismissed by reason of her pregnancy. Any such dismissal is automatically unfair and there is no two year service qualification for bringing a claim for unfair dismissal;
- to statutory maternity pay after 26 weeks' continuous employment. The maximum maternity pay period is 18 weeks. There is a system whereby the employer recoups the majority of payments of statutory maternity pay by deducting them from National In-

surance contributions the employer would otherwise have to make;

- to 14 weeks' maternity leave, and to return to work thereafter to the same job and under the same contract, for all employees, regardless of their length of service. Employees with more than two years' service will also be entitled to up to 29 weeks' absence following the birth. There are detailed notification requirements which must be complied with by the employee.

(v) Health and safety at work

An employer must take such steps as are reasonably necessary to ensure the safety of his employees. Employers who employ five or more employees must prepare a written statement of their general policy with respect to the health and safety at work of their employees and the arrangements by which this policy is to be carried out, and must bring this to the notice of all employees. The information should always be placed on an easily accessible notice board. If an employer does not comply with the requirements relating to employees' safety an employee may be able to resign and claim constructive dismissal due to a fundamental breach of his employment contract. There are also specific provisions relating to the assessment of health and safety rights affecting pregnant employees.

Employers must also ensure that people other than employees are not exposed to health and safety risks by the conduct of the business and that the premises are safe for those visiting them. An employer with ten or more employees on the same premises must keep an accident book recording specified particulars of all accidents and must notify the local authority or Health and Safety Executives of certain major accidents and specified diseases. There are also detailed provisions concerning the use of hazardous substances. If these must be used, there are control measures which must be taken by the employer.

(vi) Liability/insurance

An employer is liable for accidents caused by the acts of his employees where they are acting in the course of their employment. Every employer must insure, under an approved policy with an authorised insurer, against liability for bodily injury or disease to employees arising from or in the course of employment in United Kingdom, and must display the insurance certificate at the place of business. An employer may also take out public liability insurance against legal liability to members of the general public, as distinct from employees.

(vii) Other employment rights

English law also gives employees certain other employment protection rights. These include rights to statutory sick pay, time off for public duties and trade union activities.

(viii) Transfer of business

Statutory regulations provide for the rights of employees to be automatically transferred with continuity of service and on existing terms and conditions of employment in the event of the sale of a business (or part thereof) as a going concern. Therefore the rights and liabilities of the employee against the transferring company are automatically transferred to the acquiring company on a sale of the business. The only exceptions are certain rights relating to an occupational pension scheme. Any termination of employment which is related to the transfer will automatically be an unfair dismissal unless it can be shown to be for technical, economic or organisational reasons. Such technical, economic or organisational reasons are very narrowly defined.

The UK legislation is based on an EU Directive and applies whenever an economic activity is transferred, even where this is a small part of the overall business of the company. The UK legislation is by no means complete and it is currently being fully tested in the courts. In addition the underlying EU Directive is continuing to be extended by European Court Rulings. Every case therefore has to be carefully considered on its own facts.

Particular care has to be taken where an industry or public body decides to contract out one of its activities. The issue of the contract may act as a transfer of the business, and may also breach the EU rules for public procurement.

(ix) Pensions

Pensions is an increasingly important aspect of employment law.

Every employee in the United Kingdom who has paid the appropriate National Insurance Contributions is eligible for a basic State pension. This pension is paid as a weekly sum payable to men at the age of 65 and women at the age of 60. An employee may decide to defer taking his pension for any period until the ages of 70 and 65 respectively. The different retirement ages for entitlement to a State pension is an exception to the general rule against discrimination on grounds of sex. The pension is currently increased each year in line with the Retail Prices Index so that the value of the pension is maintained against inflation. In addition to the basic component of the State pension, is a second component known as SERPS (State Earnings Related Pension Scheme), which is a pension entitlement based on a proportion of an employee's weekly earnings over his working life. An element of protection against inflation is included. It is possible to contract out of this second feature of the State scheme, which is in any event being phased out.

Occupational pension schemes are provided by employers for their employees in addition to the State pension. The pension entitlement can either be related to an employee's earnings at or near retirement (final salary schemes) or be made up of a defined contribution (money purchase). The non-discrimination rules apply to occupational pension schemes. Such schemes qualify for tax relief.

As an alternative to an employer's occupational scheme, an employee may take out a private pension plan. The maximum contributions that can be paid into a personal pension are based on a percentage of an individual's annual earnings, the percentage increasing with age at the beginning of the tax year. The earnings on which contributions can be paid are subject to a cap or a ceiling. There are similar restrictions on employee contributions to occupational schemes.

The assets of a pension fund, whether private or employer sponsored, may be invested in any one or more of several forms, *e.g.* a deposit fund or a unit linked fund, or quoted securities.

There have been many EU Directives over the last fifteen years which are concerned with the principle of equal treatment for men and women concerning pay, which by implication includes pension rights in occupational pension schemes. This means that there should be no discrimination on grounds of sex, whether directly or indirectly, as regards the scope of the schemes and conditions of access to them, the obligation to contribute to them and the calculation of benefits.

The landmark case of *Barber* in which judgment was given by the European Court of Justice on 17 May 1990, stated that pension benefits payable under private occupational pension schemes must be equal for male and female members. This means that now occupational pension schemes must provide pensions to men and women at the same age, and that members' and dependants' benefits must be equal as between men and women. Following the recent decision in another English case, *Coloroll*, from the European Court of Justice, it is now clear that pension rights need only be equalised insofar as they relate to pensionable service accrued after 17 May 1990 until the date equalisation provisions have been introduced. For that period pension benefits must be equalised between men and women at the most favourable level. Thereafter benefits for future service could be reduced as long as they are set at the same level for men and women. As a result, many occupational pension schemes providing for benefits after this date may need to be revised to bring them into line with the position established in *Barber* and *Coloroll*.

(x) Strikes

At common law a strike by an employee is a breach of his contract which justifies immediate dismissal by the employer of the employee. In such circumstances, the employee will not have a claim for wrongful dismissal. Furthermore the employee's claim for unfair dismissal will fail provided two conditions are met: first, all employees in the employer's establishment taking part in the industrial action at the date when the individual employee was dismissed must also be dismissed; second, none of those employees can be offered re-engagement (if the employer wishes to re-engage them) until three months after the date of dismissal, or else all of them must be offered re-engagement within that period. If these conditions are not met, the question of the manner and fairness of the dismissal will have to be considered to see whether there was an unfair dismissal.

An employer does not have to dismiss in the event of a strike. Where employees are on strike or their work is disruptive, they do not have to be paid during the period for which the industrial action continues. If employees are refusing to perform only some of their contractual duties, an appropriate sum can be deducted from their wages. In practice accurate quantification of the deduction often proves to be difficult.

The law on trade disputes, strikes and other industrial action is highly complex and often connected with the law on trade union activities, the law on inducing breaches of contract, and immunities from legal proceedings. Only in some instances will it be possible to obtain an injunction preventing such action. A crucial stage where the employees are unionised, is often whether the correct procedures have been followed for a strike ballot. A ballot is not mandatory in the absence of trade unions.

From an employee's point of view the weeks during which he was engaged in a strike will not count as weeks of employment for the purposes of various statutory rights. Continuity of employment is however restored once an employee resumes work again after a strike. If an employee's continuous employment is broken, this may affect the employee's rights to the statutory claims of redundancy pay, unfair dismissal and maternity pay.

(xi) EU employment issues

The EU Commission has introduced a Social Action programme to give effect to the Social Charter which aims to improve and harmonise working conditions throughout Europe. The Social Charter has been adopted by fourteen of the fifteen Member States of the EU but rejected by the UK Government. The UK Government's stance has been formally recognised in the Maastricht Treaty where the United Kingdom has secured a right to "opt out" of future EU activities in the area of social legislation. The agreement and policies of the remaining fourteen Member States has become known as the Social Chapter.

The measures proposed under the Social Action programme are

generally in the form of Regulations, which have binding force, or of Directives, which are binding on the Member States to which they are addressed as to the objectives to be achieved, but must then be enacted in national provisions.

7. IMMIGRATION AND CITIZENSHIP

Scope

Restrictions on overseas nationals working in the United Kingdom
Investors
Visa requirements
Accompanying family members
British Commonwealth citizens
British Commonwealth citizens – working holidays
Settlement (permanent residency)
British citizenship

(i) Restrictions on overseas nationals working in the United Kingdom

(a) Background

As a general rule, overseas nationals coming to the United Kingdom to work or to establish themselves in business, require specific consent to do so. For most workers, the consent is in the form of a work permit. Consent for those coming to establish themselves in business is in the form of entry clearance granted specifically for that purpose.

The nationals of the Member States of the European Union (EU) do not require work permits or other consent to come and take employment in the United Kingdom. This is in line with the free movement of labour provisions of the European treaties.

The European Union comprises:

- United Kingdom
- Belgium
- Denmark
- France
- Germany
- Greece

- the Netherlands
- Italy
- Luxembourg
- Portugal
- Republic of Ireland
- Spain
- Finland
- Austria
- Sweden

Under the terms of what is known as the European Economic Area Agreement many of the principles of the single market are extended to Iceland and Norway. In particular, the nationals of Iceland and Norway have the same freedom as the nationals of the EU Member States to live and work anywhere within the EU. A reciprocal freedom exists for nationals of the EU who wish to live and work in Iceland or Norway.

(b) Work permits

Works permits are issued only for posts requiring:

- a recognised degree level or equivalent professional qualification; or
- senior/executive administrative skills; or
- highly qualified technicians with specialised or rare skills; or
- key workers.

People fitting within one of the above categories are expected in addition to have substantial relevant experience – for those in the first three categories set out above, this has normally to be at least two years post qualification experience.

Key workers are those who have technical or specialised skills and expertise which are essential to the day-to-day operation of the particular business. Although they need not hold high academic or professional qualifications, the employer must be able to demonstrate that the individual holds specialised skills, knowledge or experience not readily available in the United Kingdom or EU, and that the jobs of others depend on them.

There are specific rules governing the issue of work permits to hotel and catering staff and to sportsmen and entertainers.

Practical Point

Work permits for:

hotel and catering staff;
sportsmen; and
entertainers

must be applied for on separate specific forms.

Permits for entertainers are generally dealt with in the Department of Employment's "fast track" procedure.

(c) Procedure

The work permit has to be obtained by the prospective employer based in the United Kingdom. The permit is specific to the worker and to the job to be taken by him or her. The work permit scheme is administered by the Department of Employment (DOE). Application is made by the prospective employer on a prescribed form (form WP1). At the time of submission of the application, the worker should be outside the United Kingdom and it is advisable that he or she remains outside the United Kingdom until such time as the permit has been granted. With recent changes in law and the working practices of the immigration authorities, it has become virtually impossible to obtain a work permit in respect of a person already in the United Kingdom. The main exception is where the person is already in the United Kingdom under a work permit issued in respect of his or her employment with a different employer.

It should be noted that changes of employer will only be considered for the same kind of work for which the original permit was issued. Application for permission must be made by the new employer on form WP1. Similarly, if an employer wishes for an employee to change jobs within the company, DOE permission must be obtained, again by using a form WP1.

The form of application is fairly detailed and it is recommended that professional legal advice is sought.

The application for a work permit should be made no more than six months before the employer wishes to bring the individual into the United Kingdom. The DOE tends to take in the region of six to eight weeks to process applications.

In making an application for a permit, the employer is required to indicate for how long the worker is required. The permit will be issued for a specified period and the period will commence on the date the individual enters the United Kingdom.

Practical Point

It is generally the case that the worker *must* be outside the United Kingdom at the time the work permit application is filed.

It will often be necessary to advertise the position and to produce evidence to demonstrate why no suitable candidate was found in the EU.

(d) Permit-free employment – "sole representatives"

People in certain capacities or engaged in certain activities, can enter the United Kingdom for employment purposes without the need for work permits. Included in this category, are representatives of overseas newspapers, news agencies and broadcasting organisations on long-term assignment to the United Kingdom. In addition, the sole representatives of overseas businesses can enter the United Kingdom to work without work permits.

To fall into the "sole representative" category, the person must be coming to the United Kingdom on behalf of a business which has no branch, subsidiary or other representative in the United Kingdom. The business must have its headquarters and principal place of business outside the United Kingdom. The sole representative must have been recruited and employed as an employee of the business outside the United Kingdom. The sole representative must also be coming to the United Kingdom as a senior employee with full authority to take operational decisions on behalf of the overseas firm for the purpose of representing it in the United Kingdom by establishing and operating a registered branch or wholly owned business of the overseas firm (for information about the registration of branches and the establishment of United Kingdom companies, see Chapter 2).

A person wishing to come to the United Kingdom in this permit-free category, must obtain the appropriate entry clearance before travelling.

An application for clearance to enter the United Kingdom as the sole representative of an overseas business, must be made through the British embassy or consulate in the country in which the individual is then living. Certain entry clearance forms must be completed. Initially the entry clearance officer in the embassy/consulate will consider the application, but cases of this nature are often referred to the immigration department at the Home Office in the United Kingdom.

To ensure that the application is strong, the applicant should endeavour to present some form of business plan or feasibility study in respect of the proposed UK operation. This can be particularly useful if the proposals include the creation of employment (*i.e.* for persons already settled in the United Kingdom/EU) and/or involve the export of UK goods or services.

An application under this heading may be problematic if the individual concerned has only been with the overseas business for a very short period of time. The entry clearance officer will be looking to see that the individual has the requisite experience and (as indicated above) is of the appropriate level of seniority to justify his or her selection for the sole representative role. However, the secondment of the individual to the United Kingdom must not result in the overseas business ceasing to function. In other words, it must be clear that the purpose of the secondment is the commercial benefit of the overseas firm rather than the immigration convenience of the sole representative. Subject to this, there is nothing to prevent, say, a minority (but not a majority) shareholder or director of an overseas business becoming a sole representative of the business in the United Kingdom.

It is difficult to give a clear indication as to the time it will take for the authorities to process applications under the sole representative category. If the application is strong and there are no complications (such as might arise with a person with a complicated UK immigration history), the entry clearance officer should be able to process the application without referral to the immigration department of the Home Office. In cases of this nature, clearance might be given immediately, or certainly within a period of a couple of weeks. Conversely, if the entry clearance officer considers it necessary to refer the matter to the immigration department of the Home Office, there will be inevitable delays. In these cases, it can be a question of months before entry clearance is forthcoming.

Practical Point

The sole representative must be outside the United Kingdom at the time the clearance application is filed.

(e) Business immigrants

A non-EU national wishing to come to the United Kingdom to establish him or herself in business or in self employment, must hold a current entry clearance issued specifically for that purpose. The application for entry clearance must be made by the individual to his or her local UK embassy or consulate. This will entail the completion of a number of forms.

To succeed with an application under this heading, the applicant will need to be able to show the following:

- that he or she will be bringing money of his or her own to put into the business;
- that his or her level of financial investment will be proportional to his or her interest in the business;
- that he or she will be able to bear his or her share of the liabilities;
- that he or she will be occupied full-time in the running of the business; and

- that there is a genuine need for his or her services and investment.

The minimum investment for these purposes is currently £200,000. The applicant will be required to produce evidence that this amount or more is under his or her control and disposable in the United Kingdom. Evidence can be in the form of a bank statement or a bank letter. It is not necessary that the funds are actually in the United Kingdom at the time of the application. However, the funds must not be in a jurisdiction where, for example, there are exchange controls which would fetter the transfer of money to the United Kingdom.

In the case of an applicant who wishes to come to join or take over an existing business, there is a need, in addition to the above requirements, to demonstrate that his or her share of the profits from the business will be sufficient to maintain and accommodate him or her and his or her dependants. In this connection, the applicant will be required to produce audited accounts of the business in respect of previous years of trading. In addition, the following documentation will have to be submitted with the application:

- a written statement or agreement outlining the terms on which the applicant is to join or take over the target business; and
- some evidence to show that his or her services and investment will create new, paid, full-time employment in the target business for at least two persons already settled in the United Kingdom.

In cases where the applicant wishes to establish a **new** business in the United Kingdom, he or she will, in addition to the general requirements outlined above, have to demonstrate to the entry clearance officer that he or she will be bringing into the country sufficient funds of his or her own to establish an enterprise that can realistically be expected to maintain and accommodate him or her and any dependants without recourse to employment of any kind or to public funds. Here again, it will be necessary for the applicant to demonstrate that the business will provide new, paid, full-time employment for at least two persons already settled in the United Kingdom.

A person granted clearance to enter the United Kingdom either to join an existing business or to establish a new business will normally be admitted for an initial period of 12 months. Subject to his or her continuing compliance with the conditions the period of stay will be extended by a further period not exceeding three years.

(f) Business immigrants under EU Association Agreements

Certain EU agreements exist for the purpose of assisting the emerging democracies of the former Eastern bloc.

The nationals of Hungary and Poland enjoy special treatment under the rules relating to business immigrants. The conditions for entry and establishment in business are similar to those set out in (e) above, but there is no set minimum level of investment (the investment must just be "sufficient"), and no requirement that the enterprise must create employment opportunities.

Where the enterprise is established through the medium of a company, the nationals of Hungary and Poland enjoy equal special treatment. However, where the business is in the form of self-employment or partnership, the special provisions apply to the nationals of Poland only.

Practical Point

The business immigrant must be outside the United Kingdom at the time the entry clearance application is filed.

Except in the case of Hungarian and Polish nationals the minimum personal investment is currently £200,000.

(g) Business visitors

Visitors to the United Kingdom are entitled to transact business while there. However, great care must be exercised to ensure that a business visit does not develop into a more permanent arrangement which will bring it into the business immigrant category or result in the individual requiring a work permit or other entry clearance.

A typical business visit would be one involving attendance at meetings and conferences, or perhaps the arrangement of deals and signing of contracts. However, in certain circumstances, business visits can go further than this, to include workers employed and paid by overseas companies who are sent to the United Kingdom for short periods to instal, erect, repair or service foreign-made machinery or equipment.

A business visit should not last for more than a couple of weeks, although there is no hard or fast rule for the period of time. The important factor is that the individual must not become involved directly in productive work or take up what is, in effect, a job that would otherwise be offered to someone from the resident labour force.

It is recommended that an individual travelling to the United Kingdom for the purposes of a business visit should endeavour to keep his or her time in the United Kingdom to a minimum and should be in possession of a letter from his or her employer outlining the purpose of the visit together with a return travel ticket. Professional advice should be sought as to the contents of the letter.

Although there is no requirement for a business visitor to obtain entry clearance for the United Kingdom, some nationals will require visas (see (iii) below).

(ii) **Investors**

This category presents the opportunity for an individual to apply for admission to the United Kingdom as an investor.

To succeed with an application for entry clearance under this category the applicant must be able to demonstrate that he or she:

- has money of his or her own (under his or her control) and disposable in the United Kingdom amounting to no less than £1 million; and
- intends to invest not less than £750,000 in the United Kingdom by way of UK Government bonds, share capital or loan capital, in active, trading UK registered companies (but not those principally engaged in property investment, and excluding investment by way of deposits with banks, building societies or similar organisations); and
- intends to make the United Kingdom his or her main home; and
- is able to maintain and accommodate himself or herself and any dependants without taking employment (other than self-employment or business) or recourse to public funds.

A person qualifying under this category will normally be admitted to the United Kingdom for an initial period of 12 months. Subject to compliance with the conditions, that period of stay will be extended by a further period not exceeding three years.

(iii) **Visa requirements**

The nationals of certain countries and territorial entities require visas for entry into the United Kingdom irrespective of the purpose of their visit.

A visa application must be made to the person's nearest British High Commission, embassy or consulate.

The nationals of the following countries or territorial entities require visas for the United Kingdom:

Afghanistan
Albania
Algeria
Angola
Armenia
Azerbaijan
Bangladesh
Belarus
Benin
Bhutan
Bosnia-Herzegovina
Bulgaria
Burkina
Burma
Burundi
Cambodia
Cameroon
Cape Verde
Central African Republic
Chad
China
Comoros
Congo
Cuba
Djibouti
Gabon
Georgia
Ghana
Guinea
Guinea-Bissau
Haiti
India
Indonesia
Iran
Iraq
Ivory Coast
Jordan
Kazakhstan
Kirgizstan
Korea (North)
Laos
Lebanon
Liberia
Libya
Macedonia
Madagascar
Mali
Mauritania
Moldova
Mongolia
Oman
Pakistan
Philippines
Romania
Russia
Rwanda
Sao Tome e Principe
Saudi Arabia
Senegal
Sierra Leone
Somalia
Sri Lanka
Sudan
Syria
Taiwan
Tajikistan
Thailand
Togo
Tunisia
Turkey
Turkmenistan
Uganda
Ukraine
Uzbekistan
Vietnam

Egypt
Equatorial Guinea
Erikea
Ethiopia
Morocco
Mozambique
Nepal
Nigeria
Yemen
Zaire

Nationals of the territories formerly comprising the Socialist Federal Republic of Yugoslavia excluding Croatia and Slovenia and persons who hold passports or travel documents issued by the former Soviet Union or by the former Socialist Federal Republic of Yugoslavia also require visas for the United Kingdom.

Practical Point

The schedule of 'visa countries' is subject to change at very short notice. Accordingly, it is advisable to check the requirements before any travel.

Medical

A person who intends to remain in the United Kingdom for more than six months may be referred to the government medical inspector for examination.

(iv) Accompanying family members

The spouse and dependant unmarried children under eighteen years of age of a person admitted to the United Kingdom (for the purposes of employment under a work permit; or in the permit-free category, or for the purposes of establishment in business, or as an investor) will normally be given leave to enter for the period of that person's authorised stay. However, the spouse and children will require specific entry clearance. The entry clearance must be applied for through the relevant British High Commission, embassy or consulate.

The entry clearance officer will refuse entry clearance unless he is satisfied that there will be adequate accommodation for the family without recourse to public funds and that they will be able to maintain themselves adequately.

It is generally the case that a child will not be admitted to join or accompany a parent if the spouse of that parent is not also admitted.

No other dependant (such as a parent or grand-parent) will be admitted before the person is settled here (see (vii) below).

(v) British Commonwealth citizens

Where a Commonwealth citizen (aged 17 or over) can produce evidence that one of his or her grand-parents was born in the United Kingdom and that he or she intends to take or seek employment in the United Kingdom, and that he or she will be able to accommodate him or herself and any dependants adequately without recourse to public funds, he or she will be granted entry clearance to take or seek employment in the United Kingdom. There will be no need for the individual to obtain a work permit.

A person admitted in this category will normally be given leave to remain for a period of four years. At the end of that period, the person will be able to apply for indefinite leave to remain.

(vi) British Commonwealth citizens – working holidays

Commonwealth citizens aged between 17 to 27 (inclusive) who wish to enter the United Kingdom for an extended holiday before settling in their own countries will normally be admitted for a period of up to two years. However, a person applying for entry clearance under this particular category will need to show that they will not become a burden on public funds and that they have the means to pay for their return journey. A person admitted in this category is entitled to take employment, but on the understanding that any such employment is incidental to their extended holiday.

(vii) Settlement (permanent residency)

Where a person has remained in the United Kingdom for the purposes of approved employment (*i.e.* under a work permit), permit-free employment, as a business immigrant or in self employment, or as an investor, for a total of four years, he or she may, on application, have the time limit on his or her stay removed. This position of indefinite leave to remain is known as settled status.

The grant of settled status is not automatic and is always within the discretion of the immigration authorities. However, if the individual has not breached the terms of his or her leave to remain and has generally been a good citizen, there should be no real difficulty in securing settled status. Occasionally difficulties can arise where an individual has, during the four-year period, spent substantial periods of time outside the United Kingdom. With the nature of some businesses, long periods of travel abroad are inevitable, but if it can be shown that the international travel was for the benefit of the business, it will normally be possible to overcome any initial rejection by the immigration authority. In cases where the settled status is rejected, a further period of leave to remain will normally be granted by the immigration authority and the individual will have the option of reapplying for settled status at a later date.

(viii) British citizenship

On completion of a period of five years residency in the United Kingdom, a person has the basis from which to apply for naturalisation as a British citizen.

The five-year residency requirement is fulfilled if the person:

- was in the United Kingdom at the beginning of the five-year period (this is the period ending with the day on which the naturalisation application is received by the Home Office Nationality Department);
- in the five-year period, was not absent from the United Kingdom for more than an aggregate period of four hundred and fifty days;
- in the last twelve months of the five-year period was free of conditions under immigration law and was not absent from the United Kingdom for more than ninety days; and
- was not at any time in the five-year period in the United Kingdom in breach of the immigration laws.

It will be appreciated from this that a person who has gained settled status under the terms indicated above may (subject to not having breached the stated periods of absence or any provision of the immigration rules) have the opportunity to apply for naturalisation as a British citizen.

It should be noted that naturalisation is always within the discretion of the Home Secretary.

The processing time for naturalisation applications tends to vary but is usually from twelve to eighteen months. Once naturalised, a British citizen is entitled to a British passport.

Children under the age of eighteen years can be included on a parent's naturalisation application.

It is important to note that the acquisition of British citizenship sometimes operates as an automatic loss of a person's previous nationality. Although the United Kingdom recognises the concept of dual citizenship, many countries do not. The implications of lost nationality can be significant. For example, the loss of some nationalities can prejudice inheritance entitlement.

8. PROTECTION OF INTELLECTUAL PROPERTY

Outline Intellectual property is protected in the United Kingdom under the laws relating to trade marks, patents, copyright, industrial designs and confidential information.

Scope

EU law and intellectual property
Trade mark law
Registered trade marks
Passing off
Patent law
Industrial designs
Registered designs
Design right (unregistered designs)
Copyright law
Entertainment law
Confidential information

(i) EU law and intellectual property

There is a potential for conflict between intellectual property rights and two of the fundamental objectives of the European Union – the encouragement of fair competition and the free movement of goods and services throughout the European Union.

Agreements relating to intellectual property rights, like any other agreement between parties of sufficient size and market share, will be anti-competitive and hence void if they affect trade between Member States and aim to or in fact affect free competition within the EU (see Chapter 12).

Intellectual property rights are essentially national rights, and the conflict lies in their tendency to divide up the EU by the way they are frequently exercised. Therefore, they may fall foul of the free movement provisions. Licensing arrangements for example, are only allowed to impose certain limited, territorial restrictions.

A balance has to be struck between fair protection for the essential subject matter of the intellectual property right, and the principles of EU law. For example, the owner of a patent can use his right to prevent unauthorised production of his patented product in a Member State in which he owns the patent. However, if he has already authorised production of his patented product elsewhere in the EU, he has "exhausted" his right, and he cannot prevent the import of that authorised product into another Member State where he also has patent rights.

Practical Point

The foreign investor should be aware that agreements which fall foul of EU law may be found void and unenforceable, and may also result in potentially heavy fines to both contracting parties. Professional legal advice should always be sought.

(ii) Trade mark law

Among a business's most valuable assets are its trading names, brand names, trading logos and general trading style. Such assets can be protected in the United Kingdom in two main ways: by applying to register them as registered trade marks, or under the common law action of passing-off, which is similar to the law of unfair competition in other jurisdictions. Logos and distinctive scripts may also be protected by copyright.

The law on trade marks in the United Kingdom is contained in the Trade Mark Act 1994 (the "1994 Act") which came into force in the United Kingdom on 31 October 1994, and in the common law action of passing-off. The 1994 Act replaces the Trade Marks Act 1938. The 1994 Act implements the EU Trade Mark Directive in the United Kingdom. The purpose of the Directive is to harmonise the law on registered trade marks throughout the EU. In some circumstances it will be necessary to consider the old law, but for the purposes of this overview only the position under the 1994 Act will be discussed.

Registration of a trade mark is not compulsory although registration confers a statutory monopoly in the use of that trade mark in relation to the goods or services for which it is registered. An action for infringement by the owner of a registered mark is a much simpler action than seeking recourse under the common law by means of a passing-off action.

(iii) **Registered trade marks**

(a) Who may register?

Any person, partnership or company, whether resident in the United Kingdom or not, can apply to register a trade mark, provided that the trade mark is being used by the applicant or with his consent, or that the applicant has a genuine intention to use the mark. An application is made to the UK Trade Marks Registry (a division of the UK Department of Trade and Industry). The name and address of the applicant, a statement of goods or services in relation to which the trade mark is used or proposed to be used, a representation of the trade mark and the application fee must be sent with the application. Where an applicant has no place of business in the United Kingdom, an address for service in the United Kingdom must be given.

If an applicant has filed an application in a Paris Convention country, and within six months files an application for the same trade mark in the United Kingdom, then by virtue of the provisions of the Paris Convention, the date of filing of the UK application is deemed to be the earlier date of filing of the foreign application. This is a useful means of claiming priority over other UK applications.

(b) What can be registered?

All applications to register a trade mark in the United Kingdom are examined by the Trade Marks Registry to verify that the trade mark qualifies for registration under the 1994 Act. The Registrar can reject an application if amongst other things the mark in question is not distinctive, if it is descriptive, or if it is a mark which has become commonplace in the trade in question. These objections can be overcome if the mark applied for has become distinctive through use.

The Trade Marks Registry also carries out a search of its records to see if there are any earlier registrations or applications which block the path of the application.

A trade mark has to satisfy two tests to be registrable as a trade mark:

- it must be capable of being represented graphically; and
- it must be capable of distinguishing the applicant's goods or services from the goods or services of other businesses.

It is possible to file applications for words, designs, three dimensional shapes, colours, and possibly sounds and smells, provided that such marks can be represented graphically and distinguish the applicant's goods or services.

After acceptance by the Registry, a trade mark is advertised in the Trade Marks Journal, giving third parties a limited period to oppose the registration of the mark. Any person may submit written observations to the Trade Marks Registry as to why the application in question should not be registered. This is an extremely useful way trade mark owners and others can object to confusingly similar applications filed by third parties.

Practical Point

- It may now be possible in the United Kingdom to get a trade mark registration for a 3D shape and possibly even sounds and smells.
- Under the old law an application to register a trade mark had to be in respect of goods or services falling in **one** class only of the forty two classes established by the International Classification of Goods and Services. If an applicant's goods or services fell within several classes, several applications had to be filed. This procedure has been simplified under the new law so that one application can be filed covering several classes.

(c) Duration and renewal

After initial registration a trade mark lasts for ten years from the date of filing of the application. The registration may be renewed indefinitely thereafter for further periods of ten years upon payment of renewal fees.

(d) Exclusive rights

Valid registration of a trade mark confers on the owner the exclusive right to the use of the trade mark in relation to those goods or services for which it is registered.

(e) Infringement

The proprietor (and in certain circumstances) both exclusive and non-exclusive licensees can take action for registered trade mark infringement.

A proprietor of a trade mark cannot sue for registered trade mark infringement until the trade mark is registered. However his rights are back-dated to the date of application so he can sue for acts which take place between the date of filing and the date of registration.

A registered trade mark is infringed if a third party uses in the course of trade:

- an identical mark on identical goods or services to those registered;
- an identical mark on similar goods or services;
- a similar mark on identical or similar goods and services to those registered

and, in the case of the last two scenarios, there is a likelihood that the public will be confused.

A registered trade mark is also infringed if a third party uses in the course of trade an identical or similar mark in relation to dissimilar goods or services to those registered, if the mark is used without due cause and takes advantage of or is detrimental to the character or repute of the registered trade mark.

The following are examples of infringing acts under the 1994 Act:

- using the mark on goods or packaging;
- offering goods for sale or supplying services under the mark;
- importing or exporting goods under the mark; and
- using the mark on business papers or in advertising.

There are various defences to registered trade mark infringement.

- One of the most important new defences is in relation to comparative advertising. A trader can use another party's registered trade mark in an advertisement provided that its use "is in accordance with honest practices in industrial or commercial matters" and the use would not take "unfair advantage of or be detrimental to the distinctive character or repute of the registered trade mark". It remains to be seen how the courts will interpret this wording.
- If goods bearing a registered trade mark are put onto the market within the EU by the registered proprietor or with his consent, then the registered trade mark is not infringed if the goods later enter the United Kingdom without the proprietor's consent unless there are legitimate reasons for him to oppose their entering the United Kingdom, for example, if the condition of the goods has been changed or impaired since they first appeared on the market.
- A registered trade mark is not infringed by a third party whose own name or address includes that registered trade mark provided the third party's use of the registered trade mark is "in accordance with honest practices in industrial or commercial matters".
- A registered trade mark is also not infringed by a third party who uses that mark on accessories or spare parts to the goods covered by the registered trade mark again provided the third party's use is "in accordance with honest practices in industrial or commercial matters".

Remedies for infringement include: an injunction; damages or an account of profits; delivery up of infringing goods; obliteration of the offending sign from the goods; and destruction or forfeiture of the infringing goods.

Practical point

It is now possible to infringe a registered trade mark orally, for example, in a radio advertisement.

(f) Assignment and licensing

A registered trade mark may be assigned or licensed. The assignment of a registered trade mark must be in writing and the registered trade mark may be assigned with or without the goodwill of the business in which it has been used. An assignment of a registered trade mark can be limited to only some of the goods and services for which it is registered or for use only in a particular area of the United Kingdom.

A registered trade mark can also be licensed either generally or for some of the goods or services for which it is registered or only for particular areas of the United Kingdom.

Practical point

If a company is a licensee of a registered trade mark, although it is no longer a legal requirement, it should apply to have its licence recorded at the UK Trade Marks Registry in order to ensure that if the registered trade mark is assigned the assignee is bound by the licence.

(g) Revocation

A registered trade mark is vulnerable to attack and can be removed from the Register if:

- it is not used for a continuous period of five years;
- the applicant had no genuine intention to use the mark when filing the application;
- the mark was wrongly registered in the first place;
- the mark has lost its distinctiveness or become misleading because of acts by the proprietor.

(h) Marking

Use of the words "Registered Trade Mark" in relation to a trade mark is optional. However, it is a criminal offence for any person to a make a representation with respect to a trade mark not registered in the United Kingdom to the effect that it is a registered trade mark in the United Kingdom. Use of the word "registered" or the symbol ® on or in relation to goods or services are taken as a representation that the mark is registered in the United Kingdom unless it is shown that the reference is to registration elsewhere and the mark is in fact registered elsewhere. Use of the symbol ™ indicates an unregistered trade mark.

Practical point

For the avoidance of doubt, as to the status of the trade mark in the United Kingdom it might be prudent to say, for example, "Registered in the USA" or ® USA if the mark is registered in the USA but not the United Kingdom and is used in the United Kingdom.

However, importers of products from other EU countries where there is a registration in the country of manufacture should not need to make any changes to the packaging or labelling of the product.

(i) International aspects

Owners of trade marks which are well-known in the United Kingdom but not registered, can stop the use of identical or similar marks on identical or similar goods or services in the United Kingdom where the use is likely to cause confusion. This remedy is available whether or not the trade mark owner carries on business in the United Kingdom, and whether or not there is any goodwill in the mark in the United Kingdom.

Practical point

For the first time UK companies and individuals will be able to apply for international trade marks. The Act allows the UK Government to make Regulations to implement the EU Community Trade Mark which would enable one trade mark to be applied for throughout the EU. No regulations have yet been made.

The Act also makes provision to give effect to the Madrid Protocol which would enable the international trade mark registration system set up under the Madrid Agreement to be extended to the United Kingdom. One application could cover a host of countries outside the EU and would be of great assistance to trade mark owners in an increasing international marketplace. No provision as yet has been made to implement this Protocol in the United Kingdom.

(iv) Passing off

Trade marks (both registered and unregistered) may be protected under the common law of passing off. Generally the common law will prevent one trader expressly or impliedly representing that his goods and services are connected with or approved by another trader. Use of another's trade mark is one way of making such a representation.

In order to succeed in an action for passing off the plaintiff must establish:

- a reputation in the trade mark in question, so that members of the public associate the mark with his goods and/or services;
- actual confusion, or the likelihood of confusion, by members of the public as between the infringing goods/services and the plaintiff's goods/services; and
- damage.

This makes such actions more expensive than actions for infringement of registered trade or service marks. Accordingly, registration of marks is to be preferred.

(v) Patent law

(a) General

For all patents applied for and granted after 1 June 1978, the law relating to patents in the United Kingdom is found in the Patents Act

1977. Patents which were applied for or granted before 1 June 1978 are regulated by the Patents Act 1949 (except with respect to infringement).

The Act was passed in order to bring UK law into line with the European Patent Convention and certain parts of the Act are stated to be drafted with a view to compliance with that convention. Thus, for a full interpretation, the provisions of the convention should be considered.

Practical Point

Unlike the position in the United States, patents in the United Kingdom are granted on a "first to file" basis not a "first to invent" basis.

(b) What can be patented

Patents are available for inventions only, but not all inventions qualify for the grant of a patent. To be patentable, an invention must:

- be new, that is, it must not (subject to some minor exceptions) have been made public in any way anywhere in the world before the filing date or earlier priority date;
- involve an inventive step. An invention is deemed to involve an inventive step if it is not obvious to a person skilled in the art or science to which the invention relates, having regard to all the prior art;
- be capable of industrial application, *i.e.* be made or used in industry;
- not be "excluded". "Excluded inventions" include a mere discovery, scientific theory, mathematical methods, computer programs, methods for performing a mental act, playing a game or doing business, a new animal or plant variety, a method of treatment of the human or animal body by surgery or therapy, a method of diagnosis, or any invention which would generally be expected to

encourage offensive, immoral or anti-social behaviour. Certain plant varieties may be protected under the Plant Varieties and Seeds Act 1964.

(c) Who may apply for a patent

An invention belongs to the inventor or inventors unless his or their rights have been passed on to someone else whether by law, contract, or otherwise. A patent may be granted to the owner or the person to whom ownership has passed. A non-UK resident must provide an address for service in the United Kingdom.

Inventions made by employees will belong to their employer if made in the course of employment and part of that employee's normal duties. Otherwise the invention belongs to the employee. Any contractual provision which seeks to alter the position on ownership of inventions between employer and employee is unenforceable.

The 1977 Act contains provisions whereby an employee who has made an invention which proves to be of outstanding benefit to his employer may claim compensation.

(d) Obtaining a patent

A UK patent can be obtained in one of three ways:

- a national application (to the UK Patent Office);
- an application to the European Patent Office under the European Patent Convention (EPC) designating the United Kingdom;
- an application under the Patent Co-operation Treaty (PCT) designating the United Kingdom.

Once granted, patents obtained under either the EPC or PCT become subject to the same law as a national patent.

(e) Priority

The priority date of the patent will be the filing date of the application, unless the date of an earlier application in the United Kingdom, the European Patent Office or in a Patent Convention country is claimed. To claim the date of an earlier application as the priority date of a patent, the earlier application must have been made within the twelve months prior to the filing date.

(f) Duration

Once granted, unless revoked, a UK patent lasts for a maximum of twenty years from the filing date (for pharmaceutical patents, see below). Renewal fees become payable at the beginning of the fifth year. A patent will lapse if the renewal fees are not paid.

(g) Patent owner's rights

A patent gives the patent owner the exclusive right to manufacture, use, import, sell or otherwise dispose of the patented invention. A patent is not enforced automatically. It is the responsibility of the patent owner to pursue infringers.

A person infringes a patent by, amongst other things:

- making, disposing, offering to dispose, using, importing, or keeping the patented product;
- using or offering the patented process with the knowledge actual or imputed that such use would constitute an infringement; or
- disposing of, offering to dispose of, using or importing any product obtained directly by means of a patented process or by keeping any such product.

There are also provisions dealing with contributory infringement. A person is a contributory infringer if he supplies or offers to supply the essential elements of a patented invention, if he knew or if it is obvious that the purpose of the supply is to infringe the patent.

Remedies for infringement include an injunction, damages or an account of profits, delivery up and destruction of the infringing goods. Where an infringement (or threat of it) occurs, a patentee may seek an immediate injunction. This will restrain the infringer's act until full trial.

(h) Revocation

A patent may be revoked (upon application to the court or the Patent Office) on a number of grounds. The main grounds are:

- the invention is not new;
- the patent does not disclose an inventive step; or
- the patent specification does not disclose clearly and completely enough the inventive step for it to be performed by a person skilled in the relevant field.

(i) Licensing and assignment

A patent may be assigned or licensed. To be valid an assignment of a patent must be in writing and signed by both the assignee and assignor. A licence of a patent (either exclusive or non-exclusive) need not be in a particular form. An oral licence will be enforceable but in view of the problems of uncertainty in construing oral contracts it is advisable for all licences to be in writing.

An assignment or licence of a patent should be recorded at the UK Patent Office to ensure that it is effective against third parties. Damages for infringement (or an account of profits) will be unavailable to the proprietor of a patent or an exclusive licensee unless the assignment or licence is registered at the Patent Office within six months of its date.

Practical point

Companies granting or accepting licences of UK patents should seek professional legal advice, as such agreements may fall foul of EU law or competition law in the United Kingdom.

In addition, a term in a contract to supply a patented product or to license a patented process is void if the supplier or licensor requires anything other than the patented product or process to be supplied by him or his nominee. Also void are any terms which preclude a licensee from using or taking competing technology. So long as such a term exists it is a defence to an infringement action brought by the patentee.

(j) Compulsory licensing and licences of right

There are provisions dealing with compulsory licences and licenses of right in certain circumstances.

(k) Marking

There is no legal requirement for patented products to be marked. However, it is an offence to mark products as patented when no application has been made or an application or patent has lapsed.

(l) Pharmaceutical patents

Supplementary Protection Certificates (SPCs) for medicinal products became available in the United Kingdom on 2 January 1993. SPCs effectively extend the monopoly protection period of patents for new medicinal products by a maximum of five years, but only up to fifteen years from the date of the first regulatory approval of the pharmaceutical product in one or more Member States of the EU. SPCs take effect on the expiry of the basic patent. SPCs do not arise automatically, it is necessary to make an application.

(m) Biotechnological inventions

A large number of applications have been made in the last few years for patents arising out of biotechnological research and development.

Although all the general provisions of patent law apply (as described above), patent applications for biotechnological inventions, because of their nature, face some specific hurdles.

For example, the European Patent Office ("EPO") had to consider whether to grant a patent for the Oncomouse, a mouse developed at Harvard University whose offspring develop tumours soon after birth. Overruling objections, including first, that the patent should not be granted on grounds of morality, and secondly, that it was an "animal variety" and therefore unpatentable, the EPO granted the patent.

In 1993, the UK High Court showed themselves to be sympathetic to biotechnology patents. In both *Chiron Corporation and Others* v. *Organon Ltd & Others* and *Biogen Inc* v. *Medeva plc* (both heard in 1993), the Patents Judge, Aldous J found the patents which related to Hepatitis C Virus (Chiron) and Hepatitis B Virus (Biogen) were valid and had been infringed. However, both cases are now subject to appeal.

Given time, therefore, as more biotechnology patents are granted and some are subsequently litigated, the ambit of patent protection for biotechnological inventions will become clearer.

The European Commission's Draft Directive on biotechnological inventions, which had been first proposed in 1988, was rejected in March 1995 by the European Parliament. At the time of writing, it is not known whether the Commission will propose a new version.

(vi) **Industrial designs**

Copyright in design drawings, for anything other than artistic work, will not be infringed by a three dimensional copy of the design drawing. Industrial designs are now protected either by registration under the Registered Designs Act 1949 (as amended), or by means of the unregistered design right under the Copyright, Designs and Patents Act 1988 ("CDPA").

Practical point

The provisions governing industrial designs and design drawings created before 1 August 1989 are complicated and legal advice should be sought.

(vii) Registered designs

Registration of a design under the Registered Designs Act 1949 protects the appearance of an article, that is its shape and/or surface pattern. A registered design gives the owner the exclusive right to the design in the United Kingdom.

(a) Registration

A design, to be registerable, must be novel and contain or consist of a feature of shape, configuration, pattern or ornament applied to an article by an industrial process. Such features of the design must be aesthetic to some significant degree. The novelty requirement is not met where the design to be registered differs only in immaterial detail, or in features which are variants commonly used in the trade, from a design previously registered or published.

Designs of certain types are specifically excluded from registration. These include:

- a method or principle of construction;
- features of the shape or configuration of an article which are dictated solely by the article's function or are dependent upon the appearance of another article of which the article is intended to form an integral part ("must–match" exclusion);
- works of sculpture (other than casts used or intended to be used as models to be multiplied by an industrial process), mural tablets, medals, or printed matter of essentially literary or artistic character.

In general only the author of the design or his assignee may apply for registration. A design made by an employee in the course of employment will belong to the employer. A foreigner may apply for registration but applicants not residing in the United Kingdom must give an address for service within the United Kingdom.

(b) Duration

Registration lasts initially for five years and is renewable for further five year terms up to a maximum of twenty-five years from the initial filing date.

(c) Infringement

Infringing acts include the making or importation for sale or hire, or for use in the course of trade or business, of an article, in respect of which the design is registered, and to which that design or a design not substantially different from it has been applied. The sale, letting for hire or offer or exposure for sale or hire of any such article is also an infringement. Contributory infringement includes making anything which enables the infringing article itself to be made.

Remedies for infringement include an injunction, damages or an account of profits, and delivery up and destruction of the infringing articles.

(d) Assignment

A registered design may be wholly or partially assigned. The assignment must be registered.

(e) Marking

There is no legal requirement to mark articles, but where there is no marking, in proceedings for infringement of a registered design, damages will not be awarded against a defendant who proves that at the time of the infringement, there were no reasonable grounds to suppose that the design was registered. It is, therefore, advisable to apply the words "registered" together with the registration number.

(viii) Design right (unregistered design)

Design right can be obtained in respect of a new and original design, that is a design which is not commonplace in the relevant design field at the time of its creation, under the CDPA. "Design" is defined as the design of any aspect of the shape or configuration (whether internal or external) of the whole or part of an article.

Design right is obtained without registration and originates at the time the design is first recorded in a "Design Document" (this may be a drawing, photograph, written description, or data stored in a computer) or at the time an article is made up to the design, whichever is the earlier.

Design right does not subsist in those aspects of the design which enable the article to be connected to, or placed in, around or against another article so that either article may perform its function (must-fit), or in those features of the shape or configuration of an article which are dependant on the appearance of another article of which the article is intended by the design to form an internal part (must-match), or in the surface decoration of an article.

Practical point

A recent case in the United Kingdom suggests that spare parts for products ranging from computers to cars may not be entitled to design protection. The case is currently under appeal to the House of Lords.

(a) Duration

Generally design right lasts for either: fifteen years from the end of the calender year in which the design was first recorded in a Design Document or an article was first made up to the design (whichever is the earlier); or for ten years from the end of the calendar year in which products made to the design were first marketed.

Licences of right are available during the last five years of the duration of the design right.

Practical point

Companies considering the most appropriate form of protection for their designs in the United Kingdom should see how the licence of right provisions for designs may effect them. Can a competitor seek a licence or can a competitor be required to grant a licence?

(b) Ownership of design right

Design right is not available to everyone. In principle it is only available to persons in the United Kingdom, other EU states, New Zealand and the British Colonies ("qualifying persons"). The protection may be extended to designs originated by residents of other countries, but only to the extent that these other countries provide reciprocal protection for similar designs. Therefore, where protection of a design is desired by foreigners, in particular those living outside the European Union, registration under the Registered Designs Act is important.

Design right in a design generally belongs to the author of the design provided he is a qualifying person. If there is no qualifying person to obtain design right the person who first markets articles to the design in the United Kingdom or any other EU state is entitled to design right in the design (provided he is a qualifying person exclusively authorised by the author to put such articles on the market).

Design right in a design made by an employee in the course of employment will belong to the employer. If a design is commissioned it belongs to the commissioner not the author.

Practical point

Accurate records are important. Records should clearly show how and when new designs are first recorded and first marketed, to provide evidence in the event of a dispute.

(c) Rights

The owner of design right has the exclusive right to apply the design to articles. Any person who, without the consent of the owner, reproduces the design for commercial purposes by:

- making articles exactly or substantially to the design; or
- making a design document recording the design for enabling such articles to be made;

is an infringer.

Remedies available for infringement include: an injunction, award of damages or account of profits, or delivery up of infringing articles.

(d) Assignment

An assignment of design right must be in writing, signed by the assignor and in favour of a qualifying person.

(e) Marking

It is advisable to mark design right protected articles with the letters "DR", because no damages can be obtained for infringement if it is shown that at the time of the infringement the defendant did not know, nor had he reason to believe, that design right subsisted in the design to which the action relates.

Practical point

Registration of designs should be considered. Under the CDPA the increased duration of protection under a registered design is one factor to take into account when considering appropriate protection for designs in the United Kingdom. Registered designs have a maximum duration of 25 years compared with 15 years for design right (the last five years of which are subject to licence of right).

(f) Semi-conductor topographies

Semi-conductor topographies may be protected by design right. There are, however, a number of special rules which apply to such topographies. For example, semi-conductor topographies are not subject to the licence of right provisions.

(ix) **Copyright law**

(a) General

The law on copyright in the United Kingdom is contained in the Copyright, Designs and Patents Act (CDPA). Copyright is the exclusive right of the authors of certain original works, including literary, dramatic, musical and artistic works, to prevent other persons from copying or exploiting their works without permission for a period of time. Copyright arises on the creation of the work and registration is not required.

(b) International dimensions

Consideration of the copyright owner's rights in the United Kingdom alone could well be totally inadequate. The economic potential for copyright works today may, in many cases, be worldwide.

Multilateral conventions have been established to promote international co-operation. The Berne Convention which came into existence in 1886, is the primary international convention. The other convention is the Universal Copyright Convention which was formed in 1952. Most, but not all, countries are parties to one or other of these conventions. The United Kingdom is a party to both conventions. These conventions provide guidelines to ensure that participating states have certain minimum provisions in their copyright laws, and for most purposes accord the same treatment to authors from other participating states as they do to their own nationals. For example, an American author whose work is still in copyright in the USA is entitled to the same protection for his work in the United Kingdom as are UK nationals, and conversely, UK authors will be given the same treatment in the US as a US national.

(c) Ownership of copyright

The basic principle is that the first owner of copyright in the work is the author of the work, or the person by whom arrangements necessary for the creation of the work are undertaken. There are exceptions, where, for example, copyright works are made by employees during the course of their employment, in which case copyright usually vests in the employer.

(d) Duration

Generally copyright subsists in a work for fifty years from the end of the year in which the author died. This is due to be extended as a result of an EU Directive, to the life of the author plus seventy years for all European works which are still protected by copyright in any member state of the EU on 1 July 1995, and for all subsequently produced EU works.

(e) Rights

Copyright confers on the owner of the copyright work exclusive rights to do, or authorise others to do, the following acts in the United Kingdom in relation to those works:

- to copy the work;
- issue copies to the public;
- perform, show, or play the work in public;
- broadcast the work or include it in a cable programme service; and
- make an adaptation of the work, or do any of the above in relation to an adaptation.

(f) Infringement

Primary infringement in relation to a copyright work involves doing a restricted act in relation to the whole or a substantial part of the work. It is also an infringement to import, possess in the course of business, sell, or otherwise deal in infringing copies. These latter acts are known as "secondary infringements". In cases of secondary infringement, no infringement shall occur unless the alleged infringer knew or had reason to believe that the copies were infringing. Remedies available in the United Kingdom for infringement of copyright work include an injunction, damages, account of profits, delivery up and destruction of infringing copies and/or seizure of infringing copies. There are also criminal sanctions.

Practical point

The Police and the Trading Standards Departments in the United Kingdom are becoming more and more used to prosecuting offenders where copyright has been infringed for commercial reward. The powers of the police and (under amendments to the CDPA soon to be in force) the powers of the Trading Standards Department can be used to assist copyright owners trying to enforce their copyright and design rights. Criminal remedies are available alongside civil remedies, and therefore, enhance the relief available to the copyright owner.

(g) Assignment and licensing

Copyright can be assigned and licensed, and is often subject to a multitude of complex dealings (see (ix) below) through which its owner and others seek to obtain remuneration.

An assignment of copyright must be in writing and signed by or on behalf of the owner. The copyright owner can assign the whole or part of his copyright in a work.

Licences can be granted on an exclusive or non-exclusive basis and are not generally required to be in writing, although it is advisable that they should be, especially in the case of exclusive licenses.

(h) Moral rights

UK copyright law now recognises authors' moral rights in relation to their work. These rights are personal to the author, and generally subsist for the whole of the period of copyright protection. Under the 1988 Act authors have four moral rights, the two most important of which are (1) the right of **paternity**, or the right to be credited as the author of their work (the right must first be asserted by the author in writing), and (2) the right of **integrity**, or the right to object to certain types of distortion to their work amounting to derogatory treatment. Moral rights are personal and cannot be assigned, but they can be waived in writing.

(i) Databases

Databases whether in hard copy or electronic format are currently capable of protection in the United Kingdom as literary works (compilations). However, the proposed new Database Directive issued by the EU may remove some electronic databases (*i.e.* those whose compilation involves purely mechanical work and no element of selection or creativity) from the ambit of protection. Such databases may receive the protection of a new unfair extraction right which it is currently proposed will last for fifteen years. As currently formulated that new right will only apply to databases created by EU nationals, or by their European employers, or by entities habitually resident in the EU. The right will be renewable on any substantial change to the database.

(j) Information technology

Computer software is protected by UK copyright law as a literary work.

(k) Multi media

The United Kingdom now has well established production facilities and studios and a large number of creative and experienced multimedia authors and programmers.

It is generally thought that the producer of a multi media product would be able to claim copyright protection for his/her work as a "compilation". In addition, if software is specifically written for the product, as discussed above, this may also be protected as a copyright work. In other cases the product may be protected as a "film".

The most common difficulties which arise in this area relate to the rights which might exist in the component parts of the multi media product, for example, third parties' rights in the music, film or text of the multi media product. Therefore, it is advisable to check ownership of all underlying rights before they are used, and if necessary to license them in.

(x) Entertainment law

(a) General

Entertainment usually consists of performances of musical or literary works live, in sound recordings, films, videos, broadcasts, or cable transmissions. The creation and exploitation of these are governed by the provisions of copyright law discussed above as well as some specific provisions discussed here and the law of contract.

(b) Ownership of copyright

Generally copyright in a song (a musical and a literary work) is initially owned by the author(s), who may also be the performer(s). It may be assigned by contract in whole or in part by the author to a music publisher. Generally copyright in a sound recording or film is initially owned by the producer. In accordance with the EU Rental and Lending Directive, the director of a film or audio-visual work has to be considered as an author. The CDPA also confers rights on performers.

(c) Duration

Whilst copyright in works subsists for the life of the author plus fifty years (this will be extended to seventy years by the EU Duration Directive which is due to be implemented in July 1995), the rights in sound recordings and films expire 50 years from the end of the year of manufacture or release.

(d) Rights

The exclusive right to do or authorise copying which includes:

- the graphic right (to make sheet music);
- the mechanical right (to make sound recordings);
- the dubbing right (to copy a sound recording or film);
- the synchronisation right (to reproduce musical work or sound recording together with visual images);
- the performing right (to perform or show the work in public); and
- the broadcasting right (to broadcast or include in a cable service).

(e) Administration of rights

Rights are generally administered collectively. Rights holders assign or license the relevant rights to collecting societies, which grant licences and collect royalties on standard terms, and protect the interests of the rights holders (*e.g.* by taking action against piracy and copyright infringement).

The Performing Right Society (PRS) administers the public performance and broadcasting of its members' musical works. ("Grand rights", *e.g.* rights in operas, are not administered collectively.) The Mechanical-Copyright Protection Society (MCPS) grants recording licences for its members' musical works. Phonographic Performance Ltd (PPL) grants licences for the public performance and broadcasting of sound recordings, and Video Performance Ltd (VPL) grants licences for the public performance and broadcasting of music videograms.

(f) International dimensions

The entertainment industry is international: popular music and films are exploited throughout the world, the major record companies and music publishers are multinational concerns, and the collecting societies are members of international umbrella organisations and have contracts with their equivalents world-wide for royalty collection and distribution. Therefore rights must be asserted and protected under many legislations. Nearly all countries where significant exploitation takes place are members of the Berne Convention for the Protection of Literary and Artistic Works, and many countries are also members of the Rome Convention, which deals with the rights of performers, producers of recordings, and broadcasting organisations ("neighbouring rights"), having ratified the treaties and where necessary enacted the appropriate domestic legislation.

(xi) Confidential information

Unlike some other jurisdictions, there is no legislation to protect confidential information in the United Kingdom. The law on confidential information derives from the common law and equitable principles.

In general, information will be protected as confidential if:

- it is of a confidential nature – not public knowledge or something which is generally known in the relevant industry or trade;
- it is communicated in circumstances importing an obligation of confidence;
- there has been an unauthorised use of the information or the threat of unauthorised use.

As regards the circumstances importing an obligation of confidence, the obligation can be express (*e.g.* contract) or implied, because of the nature of the relationship between the parties (*e.g.* employer/employee, attorney/client, etc). The courts have not found it difficult to find an obligation of confidence. However, it is always preferable to have the obligation expressed, especially in the case of employer/employees, since the courts will be slow to extend implied obligations binding employees to anything other than strict trade secrecy.

Remedies available for a breach of confidence include an injunction, delivery up of confidential information, damages, or account of profits.

Practical point

The owner of intellectual property rights including rights in knowhow should not disclose information about these rights to a third party without first getting the third party to sign a confidentiality agreement. Legal advice should be sought on the provisions of such an agreement.

9. ACQUIRING PROPERTY (REAL ESTATE)

Outline

Any foreign investor establishing itself in the United Kingdom will usually wish to acquire property for the purposes of its business. In England and Wales similar legal considerations apply to the three main commercial sectors (offices, industrial/distribution and retail) and to residential property.

Scope

Finding the right property
Freehold or leasehold
Freehold
Leasehold
The planning process
Value Added Tax (VAT)
Incidental expenses on acquiring property
Residential property

Practical point

The law relating to real property in Scotland and Northern Ireland is different in many significant respects and advice should be sought from appropriately qualified lawyers if property is to be acquired in those countries.

(i) Finding the right property

There are many firms of chartered surveyors with a national network and a larger number of more localised firms who are able to co-ordinate the search for suitable premises. Once the right property has been found, it would be usual to retain that firm to negotiate the most commercially advantageous terms for the acquisition. The chartered surveyors' remuneration for this service is likely to be negotiable, but it usually takes the form of commission, being an agreed percentage of the purchase price, or initial rent if premises are to be leased.

Practical point

It is a false economy to dispense with the services of a chartered surveyor – the savings they can achieve will often outweigh the cost by far.

The location of any property acquired will be driven by two factors:

- The needs of the business – proximity to available work forces, markets or communications being most critical.
- Cost – there are significant regional variations in the costs incidental to acquiring and holding property. The principle variables will be the open market value or the open market rent for property in any particular location; and the business rates that may be payable to the local authority in that area. The actual amount of rates payable will depend upon the rateable value of the property and the annual commercial rate in the pound determined by central government.

Any of the national firms of chartered surveyors can give guidance as to the relative cost per square foot of owning or leasing premises in different areas of the country.

However, location to economically disadvantaged areas of the country is often encouraged through the medium of central government or European Union grants or by other financial inducements – for example business rate free occupation in established Enterprise Zones.

(ii) Freehold or leasehold

Since the introduction of the Law of Property Act 1925 only two forms of legal interest in real property are recognised in England and Wales:

- the fee simple absolute in possession, more commonly known as "freehold"; and
- the term of years absolute, more commonly known as "leasehold".

(iii) Freehold

In practice this amounts to absolute ownership. The owner has the right to transfer to another the whole or any part of his interest in the land and his right to everything in, on, over or under the land.

Notwithstanding the concept of absolute ownership, freehold property may however, still be subject to restrictions affecting the property in favour of other land (restrictive covenants). Furthermore, the property may enjoy or indeed be subject to rights over or in favour of other land (legal easements).

Notwithstanding the inception of universal land registration in England and Wales, the acquisition of freehold property can often be complicated and expert legal advice should be taken. Often the registration process will not have been completed, involving much more detailed work in respect of the unregistered sections on the property.

(iv) Leasehold

Leases of commercial property are freely negotiable contracts for the use and occupation of property. It became the norm for leases of prime property to be twenty-five years in length – this was driven by the requirements of the bank or institution funding the development scheme, who wished to see a guaranteed income stream covering the cost of servicing the loan to the developer.

However, the property crash in the United Kingdom in the early 1990's has fundamentally altered the balance of power between the landlord and the tenant and their relative negotiating strengths. Lease terms of fifteen years or less on prime property are now much more common. In addition, the tenant may also be able to negotiate a right to terminate the lease at pre-determined dates. It may also be possible to negotiate rent free periods and/or substantial capital contributions from the landlord.

Leases will usually be freely assignable by the tenant. However, under English law, the original parties to a contract remain liable for their respective obligations for the duration of the contract, notwithstanding assignment (the doctrine of **privity of contract**). The original tenant and any guarantor (often an overseas company guaranteeing the obligation of its UK subsidiary) can therefore be required by the landlord to make good the default of an assignee of the lease, notwithstanding that the original tenant no longer has any interest in the property. In certain circumstances, subsequent tenants can also be liable for the default of their assignees in the same way.

The recession has highlighted the harshness of this doctrine and it is possible that the UK Government may intervene in order to limit the liability of the original tenant by statute.

Practical point

If acquiring leasehold property, the investor can limit its contingent liability by acquiring short term leases. Such leases may however, be less marketable in the event of the investor wishing to dispose of the property.

An overseas company should not accept an obligation to guarantee its subsidiary's obligations under a lease. It is possible to negotiate a more satisfactory arrangement such as a deposit or bond and legal advice should be sought.

Commercial leases will normally contain the following provisions:

(a) Tenant's obligations

Among the more important obligations are:

- To pay the agreed rent – rent is usually paid by four equal quarterly payments in advance on the four English quarter days. In leases of longer than five years in length the landlord will require the rent to be increased to the then open market rent at pre-determined rent review dates. Even in today's difficult market for landlords, it is difficult to negotiate a lease where the rent may go down on rent review. Virtually all leases therefore contain upward only rent review clauses. Interest will be payable to the landlord if the rent due is not paid on time.

- To pay all outgoings in relation to the property – in particular business rates payable to the local authority and other taxes due in respect of the property.

- To repair and decorate – it will be the tenant's responsibility to keep the property in good repair and to decorate at stipulated intervals. The cost of repair can be significant and careful thought should be given to the extent of the repairing obligation to be taken on. If the property is newly constructed the tenant should insist that the landlord provides comfort from the building contractor, architect, structural engineers and other members of the professional team in the form of a warranty. This will safeguard the tenant in the event of any major defects appearing in the property.

- To deliver up in good repair – the landlord will require the premises to be handed back in good repair at the end of term, and if there is disrepair, the tenant will be responsible for the cost of making good any dilapidations (disrepairs).

- Alienation – there are normally provisions allowing the tenant to assign the lease, and possibly to underlet the whole or part of the property – the landlord's consent will be required.

- Not to alter – there may be restrictions against altering the structure or other parts of the property. Occasionally such alterations may be permitted with the landlord's consent.

Practical point

The cost of making good dilapidations can be substantial and details of the actual condition of the property at the time it is first occupied should be prepared and retained by the tenant with the help of the chartered surveyor in order to prevent extortionate claims.

(b) Landlord's obligations

- To insure – the landlord will insure the property against comprehensive risks (possibly including terrorism) for the full reinstatement value and will insure loss of rent in addition. The landlord will lay out any insurance proceeds received in reinstating any damage caused by the insured risks. The tenant will reimburse the landlord with the insurance premiums payable in respect of the property.
- To provide services – in a building in multi-occupation the landlord will provide services to the building, such as cleaning, decorating and lighting of common parts, the provision of toilet facilities and staff. In addition the landlord will often agree to maintain the roof and main structure of the building.

The cost of providing these services will usually be charged back to the tenants of the building through a service charge mechanism. The cost will vary from year to year.

Practical point

Service charge costs are a considerable exposure to a tenant and the well advised tenant may be able to limit his liability by negotiating a protection such as a service charge cap.

(c) Security of tenure

Tenants of commercial property are afforded security of tenure by the Landlord and Tenant Act 1954. At the end of the lease they will be entitled to renew their lease, unless the landlord can oppose renewal by demonstrating an intention to redevelop the property, or unless the landlord requires the property for its own use. If renewal is denied, compensation will be payable to the tenant.

In short term leases the security of tenure provisions may sometimes be excluded by agreement, although this arrangement will need to be sanctioned by the court.

(d) Licences

A building owner may prefer to grant a licence to occupy rather than a lease.

Care needs to be taken in the granting of any licence to occupy real property. A licence giving exclusive possession of commercial property for a period of more than six months will automatically afford the licensee security of tenure under the Landlord & Tenant Act 1954, including the renewal rights mentioned above.

Practical point

Do not offer short term lets to third parties without seeking legal advice. The third party may be entitled to security of tenure and the property owner may not be able to regain possession.

(v) The planning process

Before a property can lawfully be put to a particular use it must be established that all necessary planning permissions are in force.

Planning permission will not be required where the property is to be used for a use which has been in existence since before 1964. Otherwise the required use will need to be authorised by express planning permission granted by the local authority.

Changes of use from one sort of business to another will also require planning permission, unless expressly authorised by the Town and Country Planning (Use Classes) Order 1987. Other licences and consents may also be needed.

(vi) Value Added Tax (VAT)

VAT at the current rate of 17½% is payable on the purchase of any "new building" (basically any building less than three years old).

If the seller or landlord has elected to waive the exemption from charging VAT VAT may be payable on:

- the purchase price of any other property (with the exception of residential property); and

- the rents payable under a lease.

If the purchasing business or tenant is registered for VAT, any VAT paid would normally be recoverable from HM Customs and Excise. (See also Chapters 15 and 17 for VAT generally.)

(vii) Incidental expenses on acquiring property

Tax (stamp duty) is payable by the purchaser on the transfer of any real property at the rate of 1% of the purchase price.

Stamp duty is also payable by the tenant on the grant to it of a lease. The duty payable depends upon the amount of rent payable and the length of the lease. Stamp duty is also payable on the purchase of any lease at the rate of 1% of the purchase price.

No tax is payable if the purchase price is less than £60,000.

Registration fees will also be payable for the registration of any dealing with land at HM Land Registry.

(viii) Residential property

There is nothing to prevent any non-UK national purchasing freehold or leasehold residential property. Alternatively, residential property may now commonly be rented on a short term basis under the recent Housing Act. The letting must be for a period of not less than six months and the landlord will have an absolute right to recovery of the property at the end of the tenancy.

10. CARRYING ON INVESTMENT BUSINESS

Scope

(i) Overview

The United Kingdom has put into place a comprehensive scheme of regulation to protect persons in the United Kingdom who buy securities. As a general rule, any person or entity who or which sells or manages an "investment" as defined in the Financial Services Act 1986 ("FSA") must be duly authorised (effectively licensed). Hence, sellers of land or antiques need not obtain such an authorisation because their product is not listed as an investment. The sellers of a time share scheme for land, however, would need authorisation, because their product is not the land itself but rights under a contract dealing with the land. Once it is determined that investment activity is being carried out, the level of supervision, record keeping and applicable rules depend largely on the status of the purchaser. Arrangements with sophisticated institutional investors obviously need less regulation than arrangements for selling directly to the public. To the extent that any prescribed activity is carried out through another supervised party, who or which is fully regulated, the requirements can be severely reduced because the regulators already have an accountable party to ensure that all the applicable rules are being followed.

This chapter gives a summary of some of the FSA implications of carrying on business in the United Kingdom. The FSA is, however, very technical and expert advice should be obtained on any activity which involves dealing, advising, arranging or managing investments.

Practical point

As a general rule of thumb any person who maintains a permanent place of business in the United Kingdom **will** need authorisation before they conduct investment business in the United Kingdom. Persons who do not maintain a permanent place of business in the United Kingdom but still carry on investment business in the United Kingdom are known as "overseas persons" and **may** still need authorisation.

Certain activities by "overseas persons" are excluded from being investment business. Such excluded activities include:

- transactions (or dealings in investments) with or through an authorised person;
- transactions (or dealings in investments) which have not been solicited by the overseas person or have been solicited in a way so as to not contravene section 56 of the FSA (restricting unsolicited calls) or section 57 of the FSA (restricting advertising).

There are restrictions on unsolicited calls which are lifted where an overseas person calls a "non-private customer". A "non-private customer" broadly stated is either an individual acting in the course of investment business, or is a company or partnership having a called-up share capital or net assets of £0.5m or more (increased to £5m if less than 20 members).

An overseas person may also make unsolicited calls where:

- there is a legitimately established customer relationship;
- the customer relationship existed while the investor was resident outside the United Kingdom;
- the customer has indicated in writing that he envisaged calls; and
- the customer has been warned that the normal UK investor protections will not apply.

(ii) Authorisation

No person can carry on investment business in the United Kingdom unless he is authorised or exempted (section 3 of the FSA). A member of a self-regulating organisation recognised by the Securities and Investment Board (commonly called SIB) is an authorised person by virtue of his membership of that organisation. An example of a self regulating organisation is the Securities and Futures Authority (commonly called the SFA).

Practical point

A member of the SFA is allowed to conduct investment business in the United Kingdom. The SFA take a minimum of about 12 weeks to consider an application for membership.

(iii) Carrying on investment business?

There are two ways in which a person is regarded as carrying on investment business in the United Kingdom. The first is if the person carries on investment business from a permanent place of business maintained by him in the United Kingdom (section 1(3)(a) of the FSA). The second is if the person engages in the United Kingdom in one or more investment activities (which are not excluded investment activities) and his doing so constitutes the carrying on by him of a business in the United Kingdom (section 1(3)(b) of the FSA). A person who falls into this second category (and not the first category) is known as an overseas person.

(iv) Interpretations

In order to decide whether section 1(3)(a) of the FSA applies, one has to consider several words carefully:

(a) Business

The FSA does not define "business". The Securities and Investment Board have indicated "Commercial motivation is a major element of carrying on business . . . Repetition or continuity is also an element of carrying on business''. Giving investment advice on rare and isolated occasions is unlikely to be regarded as carrying on the business of giving such advice, even if there is a commercial motive. Making a regular practice of giving such advice is a different matter.

(b) Investment business

Under the FSA the following constitute investment business:

- dealing in investments;
- arranging deals in investments;
- managing investments;
- giving investment advice; and
- establishing or operating collective investment schemes.

Excluded from investment business are dealings for one's own portfolio or transactions involving large blocks of shares or dealings between participators in a joint enterprise. A joint enterprise means an enterprise into which two or more persons (''the participators'') enter for commercial reasons relating to a business carried on by them.

(c) Permanent place of business in the United Kingdom

It is immaterial where the main place of business is or whether there are other places of business outside the United Kingdom. A 1986 court case decided that the private residence of the director of a foreign company could be that company's ''established place of business''. The mere presence of a director in his English home is not enough to render it a place of business, but if there is evidence that he conducted the company's business from there, it probably is.

(d) Maintained by him

The use of the word ''maintained'' suggests that some positive activity is required by the person in relation to the premises and that the person has some responsibility for or control over the premises.

(v) Overseas persons

A person who does not fall within section 1(3)(a) but might fall within (b) is termed an "overseas person". To decide if (b) applies:

- Is the person dealing in investments, arranging deals in investments, managing investments or giving investment advice?
- Do these activities constitute a "business"?
- Does he engage in the activities "in the United Kingdom" and does he carry on the business "in the United Kingdom"?
- If the answer to the first three questions is yes, can the person take advantage of the exclusions?

(vi) Exclusions for overseas persons

Certain activities of "overseas persons" are excluded from being investment businesses. Such excluded activities include:

(a) Dealing with authorised persons

An "overseas person" who is not authorised under the FSA may still deal in investments or arrange deals in investments with or through *an authorised person*. Note that this does not apply to managing investments or giving investment advice.

(b) Unsolicited calls

Similarly restrictions against dealing in investments, arranging deals in investments, managing investment and giving investment advice do not apply (as a result of Schedule 1, part IV, para 27(i) of the FSA) to:

(a) an approach made to the overseas person by or on behalf of the person in the United Kingdom which either has not been in any way solicited by the overseas person, or has been solicited by him in a way which has not contravened section 56 or 57 of the FSA; or

(b) an approach made by the overseas person which has not contravened either of those sections.

Section 56 of the FSA deals with unsolicited calls. Section 57 of the FSA deals with restrictions on advertising.

(c) Calls to non-private customers

Section 56 of the FSA is coupled with the Common Unsolicited Calls Regulations. These provide by Regulation 1(2), that where the call is an overseas person call:

(a) the marketing restriction is lifted to the extent that the call is made with a view to the investor entering into the investment agreement as a non-private customer; and
(b) the dealing restriction is lifted to the extent that the investor enters into the investment agreement as a non-private customer.

A non-private customer, broadly stated, is an individual acting in the carrying on of investment business, or a company or partnership with net assets of £5m or more (reduced to £0.5m if more than 20 members).

Practical point

These rules are highly technical and legal advice must be sought. Criminal as well as civil sanctions are applicable.

(d) Calls to existing customers

Where the call is an overseas person call to an existing customer, the restrictions are lifted by Regulation 4, where:

(a) the customer relationship existed while the investor was resident outside the United Kingdom; and
(b) the investor has been given the prescribed disclosure.

Prescribed disclosure is described in the Financial Services Core Glossary as a written statement which must make clear:

(a) that all or most of the protections provided by the UK regulatory system do not apply; and
(b) where the business is excluded from the Investors Compensation Scheme by its territorial scope (or would be so excluded if the person carrying it on were a participant firm), a statement that compensation under that scheme will not be available;

and which may also indicate the protection or compensation available under another system of regulation.

The investor must also have indicated in writing before the call that he envisaged receiving such calls.

11. ENVIRONMENTAL LAW

Outline

The main source of environmental legislation is the EU. There have been over two hundred environmental instruments issued over the last ten years, all of which the United Kingdom has had to adopt as its own legislation. The main legislation is contained within the Environmental Protection Act 1990 and the regulations made under it. The enforcement agencies – HMIP (Her Majesty's Inspectorate of Pollution), NRA (National Rivers Authority), HSE (Health and Safety Executive), WRA (Waste Regulation Authority), and local authorities, are funded in the main by the government. It is expected within the next year that HMIP, NRA and WRAs will join up to form a unified enforcement agency.

Scope

Pollution control
Contaminated land
Liability of directors
Waste licensing
Environmental auditing

(i) Pollution control

The concept of integrated pollution control ("IPC") was introduced in the Environmental Protection Act 1990. Designated industrial processes may not operate without a consent granted by HMIP. This consent is conditional and may only be granted to those companies that can demonstrate that they are employing the "best available techniques not entailing excessive costs" (BATNEEC) to stop or to reduce emissions of specified substances into the air, water and land. "Technique" does not just apply to the process itself, but also encompasses management, training and manning levels.

Practical Point

IPC consents must be reviewed at least once every four years by HMIP to ensure that the current BATNEEC is being employed. BATNEEC is an evolving process.

Indeed, the company itself has an obligation to inform HMIP if there is a better available technique. It is a criminal offence to operate a process without such consent or in breach of its conditions.

Emissions from small industrial processes are also controlled in certain circumstances when the emissions are into air, and in all circumstances when emissions are into water. Prior consent for emissions into air are gained from the local authorities. These will have conditions imposed on them and will be reviewed every four years. The company must show that they have used BATNEEC to limit the emission to air of specified substances. Emissions to water are governed by the NRA. The NRA set water policy objectives for each water course under their control. Any authorisation must ensure that these objectives are maintained. Conditions will therefore be set on the authorisation limiting the contents of any discharge and its temperature etc. It is a criminal offence to pollute a water course. In some circumstances the NRA are entitled to clean up a water course which has been polluted and recharge the company/individual responsible. In addition they may clean up adjoining land if, in their view, the state of the land is such as to be likely to pollute the adjoining water course. The cost of this clean-up will be recharged to the owner of the land or the company/individual responsible for the presence of the contamination.

(ii) Contaminated land

In early 1994 the government issued a consultation paper "Paying for Our Past", which discussed liability for damage caused by contaminated land and who should be responsible for the cost of cleaning up historical contamination. The general tenor of this paper indicated that the government will adopt clean-up standards that will be fit for the proposed use of the land.

In November 1994 the government produced "Framework for

Contaminated Land". This is their response to the replies received in respect of "Paying for Our Past".

Under these proposals, which are not yet in force:

- Local authorities will be the main instrument for requiring clean-up of historically contaminated sites. They will achieve this through the development process by imposing a requirement on developers to produce a soil report before developing a site. The requirement will probably be imposed through the planning consent.
- The government makes it clear that the standard of clean-up will be that which is fit for the proposed use of the land, *i.e.* cleaner for housing land than for industrial development. A blanket clean-up standard (as in Holland) will not be imposed.
- A new environment agency will provide technical assistance to the local authorities, for example through the updated guidance notes of the Interdepartmental Committee on the Redevelopment of Contaminated Land. It will also have an overall monitoring role, and will report on contaminated land from time to time, basing the information on that provided by the local authorities. However, the government's requirement for a register of potentially contaminated land, by listing land which had been the subject of certain contaminative uses, is to be abolished.
- The government's policy is clear. Remedial action will only be required where there is danger to the environment or health, or where it can be done in a cost-effective manner through the development process.
- A hierarchy of responsibility is established in the paper. The primary responsibility for any contamination lies with the person who caused or knowingly permitted the contamination to occur. The phrases "caused" or "knowingly permitted" are well known to the English legal system and have been examined in previous cases. Where this person cannot be found the land owner will be required to act. However, the government state that they will introduce clarifications to ensure that the land-owner will have a limited responsibility. He will be liable only in respect of the condition of his own land and for any off-site damage which he himself caused or knowingly permitted. He will not be liable for the costs of restoring off-site damage which occurred prior to his

ownership or occupation, even where the damage had resulted from activities on the land now in his ownership. Where the original polluter has transferred his responsibilities through, for example, the conveyancing process, the enforcing authority will be able to require action from the person to whom the responsibility is transferred. This is to ensure that the original polluter does not in effect pay twice, *i.e.* by accepting a reduced sale price for the land and then through regulatory action. The government promises guidance on what is bound to be an extraordinarily difficult system. It is unlikely that it will be an easy task to show that off-site damage occurred prior to a certain person's ownership of the land, without a full soil report and environmental survey being done at the time of purchase. Some industries have for some years in this country been selling sites with a full soil survey to show exactly the state of the land when the ownership was transferred.

The government makes it clear that lenders may also in some circumstances be made liable. They will have to take responsibility where they had a "*material*" influence over the actions of the borrower.

- The government makes it clear that the lender will not be liable just through the act of lending. In addition, the lender will always remain free to decide not to execute a charge on land, and a receiver will not, just because of the receivership, be held personally responsible for environmental damage.
- It will **not** be a defence to show compliance with regulatory consents.

Practical Point

Liability to neighbours for contamination of their land arising from occupation or ownership of land is governed by case law.

A recent case, *Cambridge Water Company* v *Eastern Counties Leather Plc*, ruled that there is strict liability for damage, if the damage is reasonably foreseeable. Anyone wishing to recover compensation for a polluting incident will have to establish causation and reasonable foresight.

The courts stated that liability for contamination, particularly historic contamination, was an issue that should be dealt with by the government. The government stated in this paper that it is better to let the courts decide. Only lawyers benefit from this lack of direction.

Civil liability for damage to the environment is being looked at by the EU, who have issued a green discussion paper. The green paper suggests a strict liability regime with insurance or a compensation scheme funded by certain more "dangerous" industries. There has been no draft legislation issued as a result of this discussion paper, but civil liability systems in Europe are at the moment being compared to ascertain the viability of harmonising all systems.

(iii) Liability of directors

There is no special environmental court in the United Kingdom, liability of directors is either criminal, breach of statute, or civil, as a result of damage to third party property.

Practical Point

Directors, managers and officers may be made criminally liable in addition to any company if it can be shown that they caused or knowingly permitted the breach/incident.

(iv) Waste licensing

A new system of waste licensing came into operation in 1994. A licence, required to manage or dispose of waste, cannot be surrendered until the Waste Regulation Authority is satisfied that the site at which the waste has been disposed of is in a satisfactory condition. This may require the holder of the licence to comply with obligations in relation to monitoring and venting of gases at the site for a period of 30 years. A duty of care provision places upon any holder of waste a duty to behave in accordance with a code of conduct issued by the government.

(v) Environmental auditing

A British Standard (BS7750) concerning environmental management has been supplemented by the EU Directive on Environmental Auditing. Some major companies now, as a matter of course, report environmental compliance and goals within their Annual Report. The EU scheme applies initially only to industrial sites, and aims to facilitate the implementation by companies of a system to audit their environmental performance which is recognised by certified bodies throughout the EU. It is similar to BS7750.

(vi) Conclusion

Although the pace of change has slowed considerably with the recession in the United Kingdom, awareness of environmental legislation is now an essential part of participating in UK industry. The UK environmental sector is ripe for foreign investment by way of takeover and/or joint venture. This will interest foreign investors with environmental experience in their home countries.

12. COMPETITION LAW AND POLICY

Outline This chapter deals with the EU competition rules applying to the activities of companies trading in the United Kingdom. Two sets of competition rules may apply: those imposed under UK national law, and those by European law. European rules only apply where an agreement or practice has sufficient economic impact to affect trade between Member States of the EU.

Scope

UK rules
EU rules
Article 85
Article 86
When do EU rules apply?
Distribution and EU competition rules
Joint ventures
Infringing the rules
Enforcement of the rules
Notification procedure
Merger control

(i) UK rules

The following provisions of domestic legislation are those most likely to be of concern:

- The Fair Trading Act 1973, which provides for the review of competitively significant mergers, and enables the Secretary of State to launch an investigation into such transactions. The Secretary of State has powers to prohibit a proposed merger or to order a completed transaction to be undone. A merger qualifying for investigation by the Office of Fair Trading ("OFT") is one in which two or more businesses, of which at least one is carried on in the United Kingdom or is controlled by a UK company, cease to be distinct, *i.e.* merge, and the registered assets acquired worldwide exceed £70 million, or where the parties concerned supply or consume more than 25% of the relevant goods or services in the United Kingdom, or a substantial part thereof.

- The Restrictive Trade Practices Act 1976 (''RTPA''), which requires the registration of agreements concerning the production, supply or sale of goods or services which contain restrictions on the activities of two or more parties carrying on business in the United Kingdom. The Act exempts a number of types of agreement from the obligation to register and in other cases permits certain restrictions to be disregarded.
- The Resale Prices Act 1976, which prohibits the imposition of obligations (as opposed to recommendations) on resellers to sell goods at not less than specified minimum prices.
- The Competition Act 1980, which provides a general system of control of commercial practices, including powers to launch investigations into anti-competitive practices by specific businesses.

Practical point

Many restrictions, for example non-compete clauses accepted by two or more parties in the United Kingdom must be registered with the Office of Fair Trading under the RTPA or they will be void.

(ii) EU rules

The most commercially significant provisions of European competition law are contained in Articles 85 and 86 of the Treaty of Rome. These provisions have direct effect in the United Kingdom and can as a result be relied upon by individuals before national courts. Other Treaty provisions establish special competition rules for the control of national monopolies and state aids. Separate, but similar, competition rules apply to agreements or practices concerning coal and steel products.

The EU Commission is charged with overseeing the implementation and enforcement of all EU Treaty provisions, including those relating to competition law.

Articles 85 and 86 will only apply where the agreement or conduct is capable of affecting trade between Member States. Basic guidance on when EU rules apply is set out below.

(iii) Article 85

Article 85(1) prohibits agreements (formal or informal) between undertakings where their object or effect is to prevent, restrict or distort competition. As many standard commercial arrangements can have these effects, for example, distribution rights excluding others from distributing the products in a given territory, the provisions of Article 85 are likely to be of most practical commercial significance to all but the largest of companies.

Careful consideration will be required to identify whether apparently intra-group arrangements are caught by Article 85(1). Arrangements between a principal and an agent will not normally fall within Article 85, as the agent is regarded as an auxiliary of the principal rather than an independent undertaking.

The European Commission alone has power to exempt anti-competitive agreements from the prohibition contained in Article 85(1). It does so either by individual decision or by an automatic exemption for a category of agreements – the so-called block exemptions. A block exemption provides all the benefits of an individual exemption, but only applies to qualifying agreements which contain no restrictions of competition other than those expressly permitted in the block exemption's text.

Practical point

In many cases licensing, distribution and supply agreements contain restrictions of competition which fall within the prohibition in Article 85(1). Their provisions should be reviewed to ensure compliance and enforceability.

(iv) Article 86

Article 86 prohibits the abuse of a dominant position. An abuse is a unilateral action by an undertaking, or group of undertakings, through which it exploits its market power to undermine the maintenance of existing competition on a given market, or to prevent its future development. An undertaking will hold a dominant position where it has the power to behave to an appreciable extent independently of its competitors. Market share figures of an undertaking, in terms of product and geographic market, will be important indicators of the existence of such a dominant position.

Market share percentages of over 40% will be taken as prima facie evidence that a dominant position may exist. Market shares above 25% however, may also raise concerns of dominance, although percentage shares below this figure will be very unlikely to be consistent with such a finding. Market share figures alone will not determine whether dominance exists or not; the figures must be interpreted in the light of an overall economic analysis of the relevant market.

A company in a dominant position is in effect required to observe a stricter code of commercial behaviour towards its competitors, suppliers, distributors and in its commercial relations generally. Conduct which would be permitted under Article 85 may be prohibited under Article 86 where carried out by companies holding a dominant position. Breaches of Article 86 are not capable of exemption.

(v) When EU rules apply?

The European Commission has given guidance on when it considers EU competition rules will apply *i.e.* when trade between Member States will be affected appreciably.

The European Commission's Notice on Agreements of Minor Importance (often referred to as the "*de minimis*" notice) sets out two tests which the Commission will use to determine if Article 85(1) applies:

- the goods or services covered by the agreement (plus any other directly competing goods also sold by participating undertakings) account for more than 5% of the market for such goods in the area concerned; **and**
- the aggregate turnover of the participating undertakings exceeds ECU 300 million.

The notice goes on to provide however, that even where an individual agreement does not exceed these limits, Article 85(1) can still apply, and in particular:

> where in a relevant market competition is restricted by cumulative effects of parallel networks of similar agreements established by several manufacturers ...

It is important to note, however, that this notice is intended as general guidance. It is not binding, for example either on the Commission or on national courts, and therefore cannot be relied on absolutely.

It is essential when attempting to assess the applicability of the *de minimis* notice to identify correctly the appropriate product and geographic markets. This is not always straightforward. Failing to identify correctly relevant markets can produce dangerously inaccurate and misleading information.

(vi) Distribution and EU competition rules

These matters are considered in Chapter 2(x), above.

Practical point

It is important not to assume that standard form distribution agreements which are valid in other jurisdictions necessarily comply with EU competition rules.

(vii) Joint ventures

Joint Ventures can cause significant problems under EU competition rules. If merely a form of co-operation, they will be assessed under the rules of Article 85. If the joint venture creates, on a lasting basis, a new undertaking operating in a market from which parent companies have withdrawn, the joint venture will be concentrative and *must* be pre-notified where the provisions of the Merger Control Regulation apply.

It is strongly recommended that detailed EU competition law advice is sought early on in the process of creating or altering all joint ventures. Such advice would need to assess:

- whether EU rules are applicable;
- if so, which rules: Article 85 or Merger Control; and,
- in the light of the above, whether national competition rules may also be applicable.

With consequential regulatory procedures to be observed, the answers to the above questions can have a significant impact on the ability to conclude negotiations to create a joint venture within the timetable set by the parties.

(viii) Infringing the rules

Article 85(2) provides that an agreement which infringes Article 85(1), is void and therefore unenforceable. National rules on the consequences of infringement will apply where cases are brought before the national courts. In the United Kingdom, provisions of an agreement which infringe Article 85(1) are struck out and where this results in the whole agreement losing its economic meaning, the agreement as a whole will be declared void.

Practical point

There are considerable commercial dangers in drafting agreements which contain restrictions on a party's commercial freedom without obtaining advice on the impact of Article 85(1).

A distributor may validly refuse to observe a contractual provision contained in an agreement where it infringes Article 85(1) (and is therefore illegal and unenforceable).

(ix) Enforcement of the rules

The European Commission has significant powers of enforcement of EU competition rules. Regulation 17/62 gives the Commission wide ranging powers to:

- investigate and search for and obtain documentary evidence showing that a breach of EU rules has been committed;
- fine companies, both for refusing to co-operate with an investigation or for breaching the EU competition rules. The Commission can impose fines on infringing companies of up to 10% of their annual turnover.

(x) Notification procedure

If an automatic exemption under a block exemption is not available, the only way to obtain full legal protection for an agreement containing restrictions on competition under Article 85 will be to notify that agreement to the European Commission.

There is no obligation to notify agreements which fall with the prohibition of Article 85(1). However, where an agreement is notified, the parties to the agreement will be protected from fines during the notification procedure (provided that the notification is complete) and the agreement will acquire an informal provisional validity.

A notification requires the parties to make full disclosure to the European Commission of the agreement concerned, together with complete details of their activities, size and market position. A notification will also contain an economic assessment of the impact of the arrangements and put forward the commercial justification (within the terms of Article 85(3)) of the need for and indispensability of the restrictions.

The European Commission will consider the notification in detail and may object to certain provisions, seeking thereby to ensure that such provisions are modified.

A notification will normally be concluded informally by an administrative letter. In special cases it will be concluded by a formal decision. It will be the European Commission that ultimately decides whether it wishes to proceed to a formal decision (and will invariably do so where an agreement includes a new point of law or is the first agreement to be notified in a new sector of the economy).

Unless exceptional reasons of urgency can be shown, it may take the Commission a minimum of 12 to 18 months to deal with a notification by informal administrative decision and two or more years to deal with a notification on a formal basis. In the case of justifications of joint ventures the Commission now tries to deal with these applications within a period of two months.

(xi) Merger control

In 1990 the European Union adopted legislation to introduce a formal procedure of prior notification and clearance for qualifying mergers. The Merger Control Regulation (MCR) made prior notification and suspension of the transaction obligatory for qualifying transactions pending the completion of a preliminary competition review.

The MCR applies to both mergers and to concentrative joint ventures which result in a structural change in the market concerned.

The MCR provides that a qualifying merger cannot be implemented prior to notification or within three weeks after this date. The Merger Task Force (MTF), the specialist Commission division administering the MCR, can where necessary extend the period of suspension.

The MTF has to take an initial decision to clear the transaction or to launch a full investigation within one month of the date of notification.

Where the MTF initiates a full investigation it must make its decisions as soon as possible, and in any event within not more than four months from the date of initiation of the full investigation.

The MCR procedure only applies to "concentrations" which have a "Community dimension". A "Community dimension" exists where the following financial criteria are satisfied:

- the aggregate worldwide turnover of the parties to the concentration for the previous financial year exceeds ECU 5 billion;
- the Community wide annual turnover of at least two of the undertakings for the previous financial year exceeds ECU 250 million;

- the parties do not *each* obtain more than two-thirds of their Community wide annual turnover in one and the same Member State.

Figures for the turnover of each undertaking must be aggregated with the turnover of all undertakings controlling, controlled by, or jointly controlling that undertaking. Special rules apply for calculating the turnover of banks, insurance companies and other financial institutions.

Notification under the MCR involves the submission of comprehensive and detailed commercial information to the Commission's Merger Task Force.

Practical point

Where a merger falls within the provisions of the MCR, the only competition review will be carried out at a European level. Mergers falling outside the MCR may be subject to national merger control procedures in individual Member States.

As a result, the MCR's "one stop shop" can be a significant benefit in practice in assisting in the conclusion of a complex transaction.

The MCR rules apply to companies and merger transactions worldwide where the threshold criteria are met.

When contemplating a transaction which may qualify as a concentration under the Merger Regulation, it is important to take EU legal advice early, in order to prepare the detailed submissions in advance, and in order to be able to meet the strict EU merger timetable.

13. EUROPEAN UNION AND THE INTERNAL MARKET

Scope

Treaty of Rome
Single market legislation
Removal of barriers to trade
Protection of consumers and the environment
Public procurement
Maastricht
The European company

(i) Treaty of Rome

When the Treaty of Rome came into force in 1958, it contained binding Treaty provisions to eliminate restrictions on the free movement of goods, services, capital, and persons, in order to eliminate obstacles to intra-Community trade and thus create a common (or internal) market within a defined timetable.

Despite achieving significant progress towards achieving these objectives during the 1960s, little or no progress was made during the 1970s and early 1980s. It became increasingly clear that the single market would not be achieved without a renewed and vigorous programme of legislative measures.

(ii) Single market legislation

Renewed and vigorous input was provided by the European Commission, under the Presidency of Jacques Delors, between 1985 and 1994. A Commission White Paper setting out a detailed legislative programme to bring about the single market led to the Single European Act in 1986, which enabled so-called Single Market legislation to be adopted by a qualified majority vote in the Council of Ministers, rather than by unanimity as had previously been required. A package of harmonisation and liberalisation legislation was identified and a timetable imposed to adopt such measures by the end of 1992 in order to create an internal market. Of the 282 measures proposed under this legislative package only 18 remain to be adopted.

The most significant amendments introduced by the Single European Act were constitutional. The legislative blockage which had prevented certain important texts from being adopted, for example the Merger Control Regulation, was removed by the introduction of qualified majority voting. At the same time the European Parliament's role in the legislative process was increased to improve democratic accountability. During the course of the single market programme, the European Parliament's opinions became increasingly important and influential.

(iii) Removal of barriers to trade

In addition to the constitutional reforms, the Commission proposed detailed legislation to remove general barriers to trade, both physical and technical. Key provisions in this area included advancing progress on the adoption of common European standards, and reforming the existing European mechanism of creating such standards.

The Single Market programme also led to the adoption of Directives in numerous individual sectors aimed at removing particular barriers to the functioning of a single market in these sectors. Comprehensive European legislation has been adopted in the following areas:

- banking and financial services;
- company law;
- computer programmes and information technology;
- food and drugs;
- harmonization of VAT and excise duties;
- import/export formalities;
- insurance;
- intellectual property rights;
- public procurement;
- satellite broadcasting and communications; and

- transport, including air and maritime regulations.

(iv) Protection of consumers and the environment

The Single European Act committed the Community to ensure that in **all** legislation a high degree of protection was given to consumers and to the environment. The harmonized rules on social policy and employment law received heightened attention.

(v) Public procurement

The rules on public procurement are of particular commercial significance. These now set out comprehensive procedures to ensure that important public supply and works contracts are not awarded nationally, but are instead advertised throughout Europe.

(vi) Maastricht

Further measures to develop the concept of a single market were introduced in the Treaty of European Union, better known as the Maastricht Treaty. Among these is the highly controversial Economic and Monetary Union (EMU). The Member States have committed themselves to achieving EMU at the earliest by 1997 and at the latest by 1999. The United Kingdom and Denmark have reserved their position regarding participation in EMU.

(vii) The European company

It is ironical that at the end of the single market programme one of the most important measures which remains yet to be adopted, is the proposal for a European company, the corporate vehicle designed to assist companies and undertakings to integrate and carry on business at a European rather than a national level.

14. ANTI-DUMPING

Scope

Background
Dumping
Injury
Procedure
Complaint and initiation
Investigation
Verification visit
Provisional anti-dumping duty
Definitive dumping duty
Termination or review

(i) Background

The European Union operates as a single customs area. This means that products, once imported into the United Kingdom (*i.e.* duty paid and cleared at the port of entry), are free to move throughout the Union. Although customs classification and all trade measures are implemented at a European level, these rules are administered nationally by national customs authorities.

Anti-dumping duties may be imposed on imported products from third countries which are being sold on the European market at prices less than the comparable price paid for the products in the exporting country, provided that such exports are causing or threaten to cause material injury to the European Union industry, and it is in the interests of the European Union that such duties are imposed. The object of an anti-dumping duty is therefore to counteract the injurious impact of dumped imports and to restore fair competition.

A new EU anti-dumping regulation, Regulation 3283/94, was adopted on 22 December 1994, to give effect to changes in the EU's international obligations made under the GATT 1994 Agreement.

As with all decisions taken by European Union institutions, decisions taken to impose anti-dumping duties can be appealed to the European Courts in Luxembourg.

(ii) Dumping

Dumping occurs when the "export price" to the EU of a given product is less than the "normal value" of the like product on the domestic market. Normal value is usually determined by reference to the sale price of the product in the exporter's home market. A comparison of the prices charged in the two markets will indicate whether a dumping margin exists.

(iii) Injury

Before an anti-dumping duty may be imposed it must be shown that the dumping is causing or threatening to cause material injury to the EU industry. The impact of dumping on factors such as production, sales, stocks, profit levels and market share will be taken into account when determining whether such injury is or could take place.

Injury is to be regarded as negligible where the level of dumping does not exceed 2% of the export price. In carrying out an investigation, the Commission must satisfy itself that it is the dumping activity that is causing the injury to the European Union industry and not other factors, for example "trade restrictive practices of and competition between European Union producers and foreign producers".

Even if material injury or the threat of such injury is shown to exist, an anti-dumping duty can only be imposed where it is in the European Union's interest to do so.

(iv) Procedure

Regulation 3283/94 includes new provisions on the timetable and procedures to be adopted by the European Commission which, when brought into force, will represent a significant advance in EU anti-dumping procedure. Although the new rules apply to proceedings initiated by the Commission after 1 September 1994, provisions relating to the initiation of dumping investigations are not currently in force. A Council of Ministers decision is required to bring these measures into force, and this decision must be taken before 1 April 1995.

When these new rules are brought into force the new time limits will be as follows :

- the Commission will have to initiate an investigation or reject a complaint within 45 days of its receipt;
- any investigation will normally have to be concluded within a year and *must* be completed within 15 months;
- provisional duties will have to be imposed no sooner than 60 days after the commencement of an investigation, and no later than nine months after initiation.

(v) Complaint and initiation

Any natural or legal person may make a written complaint to the Commission on behalf of the European industry, or those who effectively account for the "major proportion" of its production. The Commission will consider the information and evidence provided, and if it considers that there is sufficient evidence it will initiate a formal investigation.

(vi) Investigation

A formal notice of initiation is published in the Official Journal, specifying the products to be investigated, the exporting countries covered, and the period to be investigated. A questionnaire is then sent to exporters and importers, who have thirty days to respond. The questionnaire asks for information on the production and sales of the products under investigation. The information requested may include commercially sensitive information, which the Commission is required to treat in strict confidence. In practice this time period is often extended to enable exporters to respond fully.

During the investigation period, parties to the investigation benefit from certain rights and safeguards:

- to have access to the European Commission's non-confidential files;
- the right to a fair hearing, which includes the right to be heard at an informal hearing;

- the right to be informed of the essential facts and considerations which the EU Commission has taken into account. Parties must request to exercise this right within one month of the imposition of any provisional anti-dumping duties at the latest. After disclosure, representations may be made as to the methodology adopted and the accuracy of the facts used by the Commission.

A failure by the European Commission to observe these rules will render any decision liable to attack and annulment by the European Court.

Practical point

The European Commission will disregard false or misleading information. Refusing to co-operate or co-operating only partially with the Commission's investigation, may result in a "less favourable" outcome than for those companies who co-operate.

(vii) Verification visit

Before concluding the investigation, Commission officials will usually visit the premises of the exporting companies to verify answers and statements given in the questionnaire. The visit may last one to three days. Acquiescence in the visit is entirely voluntary, but refusal to co-operate may result in higher duties. The European Commission will generally indicate in advance the type of information to be verified.

(viii) Provisional anti-dumping duty

Following consultation with the Advisory Committee, the Commission may impose provisional duties if the preliminary investigation shows dumping or subsidy and sufficient evidence of injury caused, provided also that such action is in the interests of the European Union. In cases of extreme urgency the Commission need not consult with the Advisory Committee. The Council acting by qualified majority may override the Commission's imposition of provisional duties. The maximum duration of provisional duties is normally six months but they may be imposed for, or extended to, nine months where the parties involved do not object.

(ix) Definitive dumping duty

Where dumping and injury have been established and the European Union interest requires intervention, definitive duties may be imposed. Since March 1994 decisions by the Council to impose definitive anti-dumping duties are taken by a simple majority, and not by a qualified majority as was previously the case.

Individual dumping duties are normally imposed for all exporting companies. Residual duty rates cover exports from manufacturers who are not given individual rates.

If definitive measures are not adopted, the proceedings may be terminated, or undertakings from the parties involved may be accepted by the Commission.

(x) Termination or review

Definitive duties only remain in force "for so long as and to the extent necessary". They lapse in any event, five years after their entry into force. Under the so-called sunset procedure, a notice of impending expiry is published in the Official Journal at an appropriate time in the final year of validity of the duties. If interested parties can show injury or the threat of injury, the European Commission may issue a notice of intention to review the dumping duty. Pending the outcome of the review, the anti-dumping duty will remain in force.

15. TAX IMPLICATIONS OF CONDUCTING BUSINESS

Scope

(i) Background

The United Kingdom offers an attractive business tax regime. In particular, the 33% corporation tax rate is, along with Luxembourg, the lowest in the European Community and the rate for small companies is lower still – just 25%. In addition, various reliefs and cash grants are available, particularly in designated development areas, to encourage new investment. (see Chapter 3 *supra*).

(a) Companies

The United Kingdom provides a favourable climate for businesses from a tax point of view and there is an extensive network of double tax treaties enabling tax efficient repatriation of profits.

There is a system of direct and indirect taxation with the principal taxes affecting corporations being:

- Corporation Tax, which is levied on both income and chargeable gains; and
- Value Added Tax, which is charged on supplies of goods and services to consumers and on the importation of goods into the United Kingdom (see Chapter 17).

(b) Individuals

The main direct taxes affecting individuals are:

- Income Tax;
- Capital Gains Tax; and
- Inheritance Tax.

(c) Other taxes

There are a number of other taxes or levies in the nature of tax which a person establishing a business in the United Kingdom will also need to consider. These include:

- National Insurance contributions, which are calculated by reference to an employee's pay and benefits, and payable by an employer;
- Uniform Business Rate assessed on the occupiers of non-domestic property; and
- Stamp Duty levied on certain documents, usually at a rate of between $\frac{1}{2}$% and 1%.

(d) Administration

UK taxation is based partly on statute and partly on case law. Although there are specific exceptions, relating primarily to the application of anti-avoidance legislation, there is no general system for the provision of advance rulings.

Most of the principal taxes are administered by the Inland Revenue, with the exception of Value Added Tax which is operated by Customs & Excise. National Insurance contributions are collected by the Department of Social Security, and Uniform Business Rate by local authorities according to the region in which the property is located.

The United Kingdom has recently introduced a Pay and File system for corporation tax in respect of all accounting periods ending on or after 1 October 1993. Tax becomes due nine months after the end of a company's accounting period and interest runs from that date regardless of whether an assessment has been made. The taxpayer must make its own estimate of the tax, and is under a duty to file its completed tax return, accounts and computations within twelve months of the accounting period. The legislation makes provision for payments on account, to prevent interest running where the final tax has not been computed, and there are automatic penalties for non-compliance.

(ii) **Liability of companies to UK taxation**

The liability of a company to taxation in the United Kingdom will depend on a number of factors including, in particular:

- whether or not the company is resident in the United Kingdom;
- if the company is non-UK resident, whether or not the company operates a branch or agency in the United Kingdom.

(a) Company residence

A company will normally be resident in the United Kingdom if :

- it was incorporated in the United Kingdom after 15 March 1988; or
- it is centrally managed and controlled in the United Kingdom regardless of where it was incorporated or registered.

Under UK law it is possible for a company to be resident in more than one jurisdiction at the same time and the mere fact that a company is treated as resident in another country by taxation authorities of that country will not prevent the company from being treated as resident in the United Kingdom if either of the above tests are satisfied. However a recent change in the law means that, with effect from 30 November 1993, a company which is regarded as not resident in the United Kingdom for the purposes of any double taxation relief arrangements will be treated as non-resident in the United Kingdom for all tax purposes.

(b) Branch or agency

A branch or agency is defined as meaning "any factorship, agency, receivership, branch or management" and it is a question of fact and degree as to whether or not a non-resident company is operating a branch or agency. It is common for companies to establish co-ordination centres or representative offices which do not carry on any trade in the United Kingdom. In general a place of business will not amount to a branch or agency if the business carried on from there is only incidental or ancillary to the business of the company taken as a whole. Examples of such operations include warehousing facilities, administrative offices and registration offices (see Chapter 2 above).

Practical point

The Inland Revenue will automatically assume that a branch office is conducting taxable business. This is not the case with a place of business unless its existence and activities come to the notice of the Inland Revenue.

It is possible for a non-resident company to have income arising in the United Kingdom without having a branch or agency in the United Kingdom. Examples of such situations include companies which own UK patents from which they derive royalties, and real estate companies holding investment properties in the United Kingdom in respect of which they receive rent.

(c) Liability to UK taxation

The liability of companies to UK taxation may be summarised as follows:

- Companies resident in the United Kingdom are liable to corporation tax on their worldwide profits (including income and chargeable capital gains);
- Companies not resident in the United Kingdom, but trading in the United Kingdom through a branch or agency, are liable to corporation tax on the trading profits and gains of the UK branch;
- Companies not resident in the United Kingdom and with no branch or agency in the United Kingdom are liable to *income* tax

at the basic rate (25% for the year of assessment 1995/96) on income arising in the United Kingdom. No tax is payable in respect of capital gains accruing to such companies, even if the capital gain arises as a result of the disposal of UK assets.

In many cases the UK taxation burden may be relieved by reason of the substantial number of double taxation treaties entered into between the United Kingdom and other jurisdictions. Each treaty is different, but the general aim is to ensure that the same income or gain is not taxed twice by both countries. This will often result in the taxpayer receiving credit for taxes paid in other jurisdictions, but being obliged to pay the balance of any additional tax if the applicable tax rate in the home jurisdiction is higher.

(iii) **Corporation tax**

(a) General

Corporation tax is charged on the "profits" of a company. This term covers both income and capital gains. A single flat rate applies to all profits regardless of whether or not they are distributed to shareholders. Profits are computed by reference to a company's accounting period (*i.e.* normally the 12 month period used for the purposes of preparing the company's accounts), but the rate of corporation tax is set annually for each financial year commencing 1 April and ending 30 March and an appropriate apportionment is made where the accounting period straddles two financial years in which different rates apply.

The full rate of corporation tax for the financial year commencing 1 April 1995 is 33%. UK-resident companies whose profits do not exceed £300,000, benefit from the small companies rate of 25%. Thereafter companies with total profits between £300,000 to £1,500,000 are taxed at a progressively higher rate until the full rate is reached. These limits are reduced if the relevant company has one or more active associated companies in the United Kingdom or elsewhere. This is fairly crudely done by taking the limits and dividing them by the total number of companies which are associated. For example if the relevant company has two associated companies the small companies rate only applies if its profits are less than £100,000

(£300,000 ÷ 3) and there is marginal relief for profits up to £500,000 (£1,500,000 ÷ 3).

(b) Advance corporation tax

The United Kingdom adopts the imputation system whereby profits distributed to shareholders attract advance corporation tax ("ACT"). The system effectively allows UK resident shareholders to offset part of a company's corporation tax against their own tax liability in respect of dividends paid by that company. The ACT acts as a double credit and is treated both as an advance payment against the company's mainstream corporation tax liability and as a credit against the shareholder's liability. The position in relation to foreign shareholders is discussed in more detail in (d) below.

ACT becomes due 14 days after the end of the quarter in which the dividend is paid, and in the financial year 1995/96 the rate of ACT is equal to 25% of the dividend declared.

Example

If a company pays a dividend of £2,000,000 to its shareholders it will have to account to the Inland Revenue for ACT of £500,000. Assuming it has profits of £3,000,000 its position will therefore be as follows:

	£'000
Profits	3,000
less	
Corporation tax at 33%	990
Net Profit	2,010
Cash	3,000
less	
Dividend	2,000
ACT (25% of dividend)	500
Balance of corporation tax	490
Net cash position	£10

- This example is for illustrative purposes and is a simplification of the position. ACT is in fact first set off against the corporation tax for the accounting period in which the dividend is paid, as opposed to that for the accounting period in respect of which the dividend is declared.
- Shareholders will be treated as receiving taxable income of £2,500,000 (*i.e.* the dividend plus the ACT) which has already borne tax of £500,000 and for which (assuming they are UK residents) they will be given credit.

(c) Limitations on ACT set off

There is an important restriction upon the ability of a company to set off ACT against its mainstream corporation tax liability – the amount which may be set off must not exceed an amount equal to income tax at the lower rate (20% for the year of assessment 1995/96) on the company's profits charged to corporation tax for that period. Application of this rule frequently gives rise to surplus ACT which cannot be set off against mainstream corporation tax in the relevant accounting period. This may occur because dividends are paid in respect of a previous profitable period at a time when profits are depressed, and there is therefore insufficient corporation tax to be offset, or because dividends are paid out of income which does not attract corporation tax (*e.g.* income from a foreign jurisdiction which has already suffered tax in that jurisdiction and is relieved from UK taxation by reason of double tax relief).

In order to relieve the burden of the above rule, surplus ACT may be carried back against corporation tax liability in respect of the previous six years and may be carried forward indefinitely. There are also more restricted rules for the use of surplus ACT by other UK resident companies in the same group of companies.

(d) Repatriation of profits

Subject to certain exceptions discussed in (e) below, a company must pay ACT on a dividend regardless of whether or not the recipient shareholder is resident in the United Kingdom. However non-resident shareholders will only be entitled to the tax credit if they have other UK income or if a double tax agreement ("DTA") applies.

Set out below is an example of the position where a UK subsidiary pays a dividend to its US parent:

Example

	£	
UK Co Trading Profit	120.00	
Mainstream Corp Tax ("MCT") at 33%	39.60	
Profit after Tax		80.40
Dividend to US Parent	80.00	
ACT (set against MCT)	20.00	
		100.00
Relevant DTA entitles Parent to repayment*:		
Half normal tax credit	10.00	
less 5% of (dividend + half credit)	4.50	
		5.50
Cash received by US Parent		
Net dividend	80.00	
Cash repayment	5.50	
		85.50
Cash Position of UK Company		
Profit	120.00	
Less: ACT	20.00	
Balance of MCT	19.60	
Dividend	80.00	
		0.40

*Under the UK/US DTA, if an individual or corporation claiming a credit pursuant to the DTA has more than 10% of the shares in the dividend paying company, they will be entitled to obtain a refund of one half of the applicable ACT, less a withholding tax of 5% on the aggregate of the dividend plus the refund. For the financial year

1995/96 this gives an effective UK tax rate of 28.75% on profits repatriated to the US, assuming the full rate of corporation tax is payable.

(e) Foreign income dividends

In 1994 the United Kingdom introduced new legislation designed to alleviate the problems faced by UK resident holding companies wishing to distribute profits generated from foreign operations to non-resident shareholders. As explained in (c) above, the availability of double taxation relief in respect of foreign profits can lead to a company having to pay ACT which cannot be relieved against mainstream corporation tax. If the company elects to pay a foreign income dividend ("FID") it may match this against certain distributable foreign profits. The ACT still has to be paid, but it may be reclaimed once the company demonstrates that it satisfies the detailed conditions which are laid down by the legislation. If an election is made, it must be made for all the shares in respect of which a dividend is declared, and recipient shareholders do not receive the tax credit which they would normally receive if ACT had been paid. Individuals are treated as receiving income equivalent to the dividend grossed up at the lower rate of income tax.

The legislation also introduces the concept of an International Headquarters Company ("IHQ"), which does not have to pay ACT at all if it elects to declare a FID, although it must still satisfy all the requirements relating to the matching of a FID with distributable foreign profits. There is a complex definition of an IHQ, but it is broadly one which has substantial foreign ownership and no more than 20%UK ultimate ownership.

(f) Taxation of a branch or agency

Non-resident companies carrying on business through a branch or agency are liable to corporation tax at the full rate on the following:

- trading income arising directly or indirectly from or through the branch;
- chargeable gains of the branch;

- income from property or rights used by, or held by or for, the branch.

The small companies rate does not apply and there is no ACT or withholding tax payable on the repatriation of profits. Expenses incurred wholly and exclusively for the trade of the branch, both in the United Kingdom and overseas, may be deducted from profits. This can include a reasonable amount of head office expenses. Expenditure may also be capable of being offset against profits of the main operation in a foreign jurisdiction and it is common for a foreign company to trade through a branch in the United Kingdom in the early years in order to be able to set off initial losses against income in other jurisdictions. However the provisions of the relevant DTA will have to be considered in order to determine the effective tax differential of operating through a branch or subsidiary and what tax advantages may accrue in the parent's own territory.

Practical point

Many overseas companies set up a UK branch to allow the losses from the UK business to be offset against the profits of the overseas company.

(g) *Changing a company's residence*

If a UK resident company changes its residence there is a deemed disposal of all of its capital assets at their then market value and corporation tax is levied on any resultant chargeable gain. There are procedures for the collection of the tax from group companies and controlling directors if the tax is not paid by the due date and the charge does not arise if the assets continue to be used by a UK branch. If a subsidiary of a UK holding company changes residence the charge may be deferred.

If a company ceases to be resident in the United Kingdom it will be deemed to have ceased trading and to have ended its existing accounting period, regardless of whether or not this is actually the case, and be assessed to corporation tax on its trading profit accordingly.

(iv) Computation of income

(a) General

Broadly speaking, a company or branch is taxable on its trading income as disclosed by its accounts prepared on a historic cost basis, subject to certain adjustments set out below. Non-trading income such as interest is usually taxed on a receipts basis.

The general principle in relation to trading income is that a company is taxable on its trading receipts less revenue expenditure. The most common adjustments to a company's "accounts profit" for tax purposes are as follows:

- depreciation in respect of capital assets is not allowable as such. A deduction can only be obtained in respect of capital expenditure through the capital allowances system (see (vi)(a) below);
- abortive capital expenditure may not be deducted;
- business entertainment expenses must be added back;
- no allowance will generally be given for provisions in respect of liabilities which have not yet arisen in the relevant accounting period; and
- a bad or doubtful debt provision is only allowable to the extent of specific debts and such provision must be justified as reasonable.

(b) Management charges

Reasonable charges for management services will usually be deductible provided that they are incurred wholly and exclusively for the purposes of a company's trade. The Inland Revenue will normally require details of the make-up of any such charges including details of the actual service provided. If they consider them to be excessive, the Inland Revenue will seek to disallow all or part of the charge, and they have power to substitute an arms length figure in the case of a payment to a connected party. In certain cases the Inland Revenue might also seek to argue that excessive management charges paid to a shareholder are not deductible and constitute a distribution attracting ACT.

(c) Transfer pricing

The Inland Revenue have power to substitute an arms length price in any transaction between a UK resident and a non-resident, where one party has control of the other, or both parties are under common control. This applies whether the UK company is a buyer or seller, and the power extends not only to sales and acquisitions but also to "lettings and hirings of property, grants and transfers of rights, interests or licences and the giving of business facilities of whatever kind".

The above provision can constitute a trap for the unwary and great care should be taken where there are inter-company cross-border trading transactions. In particular, thought should be given to whether or not there are any invisible supplies such as the free use of patent or other intellectual property rights which may cause a problem in this area.

Practical point

Where an overseas company has set up a UK subsidiary it is best to record the basis on which the UK subsidiary is going to undertake its business in the form of an inter-company services agreement. The exact method of trading to be undertaken by the UK subsidiary involves fundamental consideration of commercial and taxation issues and professional advice should be sought.

(v) **Deductions**

(a) Deductibility of interest

The rules relating to the deductibility of interest are complex. Some interest may be deducted as a trading expense and other interest is treated as a so-called "charge on income". Charges on income are recurring payments under an obligation which may last more than one year, and, apart from certain forms of interest, include patent royalties, mining rents and royalties and certain charitable donations.

The principal differences between a charge on income and a deductible trading expense are:

- trading expenses only go to reduce trading profits whereas charges on income may also be set off against any other form of income and capital gains;
- charges on income, other than certain UK bank interest, are only allowable to the extent that they have actually been paid, whereas trading expenses are normally computed on an accruals basis.

Interest as a trading expense

Short interest and interest payable to a UK bank is usually deductible in computing trading income. There is no statutory definition of the expression "short interest" but it is generally considered to mean interest on a loan which it is genuinely envisaged will be repaid in under a year.

If interest is payable to a UK bank in connection with a loan which has not been taken out for the purposes of the trade and which is not therefore deductible as a trading expense it will be treated as a charge on income.

Annual interest

Annual interest (*i.e.* any interest which is not short interest) is a charge on income. There are a number of restrictions which apply to limit the circumstances in which a deduction will be allowed. The following are the most important restrictions:

- the interest cannot be a charge on income if it would be deductible in computing income or gains;
- the payment must be in respect of a liability incurred for valuable and sufficient consideration;
- if the payer is a non-resident company operating through a UK branch or agency, the interest must have been wholly and exclusively incurred for the purposes of that branch or agency; and
- the interest must not be a distribution of the company (see below).

Additionally, where payment of interest is made to a person not resident in the United Kingdom, the interest must be paid under deduction of basic rate income tax (25% for the year of assessment 1995/96) to be deductible unless:

- the relevant DTA grants relief; or
- the interest is paid entirely out of overseas income charged to UK taxation; or
- the interest is paid to an unconnected person wholly outside the United Kingdom and is either in respect of a loan incurred for the purposes of the company's trade carried on outside the United Kingdom, or is payable in a foreign currency in respect of a loan incurred for the purposes of the trade, wherever carried on; or
- the interest is in respect of certain types of Eurobond.

Interest deemed to be a distribution

If interest is treated as a distribution it will be non-deductible and will attract ACT.

The following situations could give rise to a deemed distribution where the interest is paid to a connected party who is non-resident:

- if the interest represents more than a reasonable commercial return on capital;
- if the interest is paid by a 75% subsidiary, unless the relevant DTA contains an exemption; and
- if the company is deemed to be thinly capitalised (see below).

Thin capitalisation

Where the provisions of a DTA are applicable it will often provide that where, as a result of a special relationship, interest exceeds what would have been paid in the absence of such a relationship, then the excess will not be treated as interest. The burden is on the taxpayer to show that the loan is an arms length loan. In addition to the rate of interest and other terms which would have been agreed in the absence of a special relationship, account must be taken of whether the loan would have been made at all and if so what the amount of the loan would have been. This enables the Inland Revenue to disallow interest in respect of excessively high loans where there is no realistic prospect of repayment. The Inland Revenue generally expect to see a debt/equity ratio of no more than 1:1.

Practical point

If the overseas company wishes its UK subsidiary to pay interest on inter-company loans made available to the subsidiary from its parent company the UK subsidiary must not be "thinly capitalised".

(b) *Deduction of royalties for intellectual property*

UK patent royalties are treated as charges on income and are payable under deduction of basic rate income tax, unless the relevant DTA provides to the contrary. Copyright royalties are normally deductible trading expenses and must similarly be paid under deduction of tax, subject to the relevant DTA. Trademark and know-how royalties are usually deductible trading expenses, but no withholding tax applies.

(vi) **Tax incentives and reliefs**

(a) *Capital allowances*

General

Capital expenditure and depreciation charged to the profit and loss account are not deductible trading expenses for taxation purposes. However, the UK tax system recognises that certain capital expenditure on items used for the purposes of a trade should be deductible over a period and the system of capital allowances makes provision for this. Not all capital expenditure qualifies for an allowance and there are a number of different categories and rates of allowance. Most allowances are given as a deduction against trading income, but in some cases they are restricted and can only be set off against certain types of income. Similar rules to those which apply to the carry forward and carry back of trading losses (see section (vi)(b) below) apply in relation to capital allowances.

Scheme of allowances

All capital allowances are granted as a percentage of capital expenditure incurred. In some cases the legislation grants an "initial" or "first year allowance" (which can be as much as 100%), with the balance of the expenditure, if any, qualifying for writing down allowances over the life of the asset.

Although first year allowances have been very common in the past, they now only apply in limited circumstances and a taxpayer will usually be entitled to writing down allowances. These are sometimes granted on a straight line basis and sometimes on a reducing balance basis depending on the type of expenditure:

Example

If capital expenditure of £10,000 is incurred, for which writing down allowances of 25% are available, the position over five years would be as follows:

Year	**Reducing balance basis**		**Straight line basis**	
	Unrelieved Expenditure £	Amount of Allowance £	Unrelieved Expenditure £	Amount of Allowance £
Year 1	10,000	2,500	10,000	2,500
Year 2	7,500	1,875	7,500	2,500
Year 3	5,625	1,406.25	5,000	2,500
Year 4	4,218.75	1,054.69	2,500	2,500
Year 5	3,164.06	791.01	Nil	Nil

In those cases where a writing down allowance of 25% is granted on a reducing balance basis 58% of the capital expenditure is relieved over three years and 90% by the end of year eight.

Balancing charges and balancing allowances

Where capital allowances have been claimed, and the asset is sold at arms length for less than the unrelieved expenditure, then a balancing allowance for the amount of the deficiency will be granted. If the sale price is higher than the amount of unrelieved expenditure, a balancing charge is levied on the lesser of the excess and the amount of capital allowances claimed, and that amount is brought into computation as if it were part of the taxpayer's income. In the above example, if the company sold the asset for £500, having been entitled to writing down allowances on a reducing balance basis for five years, there would be a balancing allowance of £291.01. If however the asset was sold for £1,000, there would be a balancing charge of £208.99 which would be effectively treated as additional income of the company.

Categories of capital allowance

The rates of allowance current for the 1995/96 year of assessment in respect of the more important capital allowances are as follows:

Type of Allowance	First Year	Initial	Writing-down	Straight line/Reducing balance
Plant and machinery	-	-	25%	Reducing balance
Industrial buildings	-	-	4%	Straight line
Industrial and commercial buildings in enterprise zones	-	100%	25%*	straight line
Hotels	-	20%	4%	Straight line
Scientific research	100%	-	-	
Patents	-	-	25%	Reducing balance
Know-how	-	-	25%	Reducing balance

*If there is a 100% initial or first year allowance, then no writing down allowance will be available, however in certain circumstances it is beneficial for the taxpayer to disclaim the first year or initial allowance and claim writing down allowances instead. Accordingly a writing down allowance is provided for by the legislation in case this should occur.

Plant and machinery – special provisions

The most important category of capital allowance is in relation to plant and machinery used for the purposes of a trade. Certain types of plant and machinery, such as expensive motor cars, are excluded, and the system operates on a simplified basis so that generally each year's relief is calculated on a single figure, representing a company's "pool" of expenditure. This pool figure is made up of the written down value of qualifying assets in the pool at the beginning of the company's accounting period and the cost of qualifying assets added to the pool during the year, less proceeds of any assets disposed of in the year.

When a company expects to dispose of an item of machinery or plant acquired on or after 1 April 1986 at less than its tax written down value within a period of five years beginning with the year of acquisition, it may elect to have the capital allowances on that machinery or plant calculated separately from the main machinery or plant pool. This is called de-pooling and allows relief for an asset disposed of within the five year period to be adjusted to correspond to the depreciation actually experienced. De-pooling is primarily intended for assets which are expected to suffer rapid depreciation (*e.g.* because of technical obsolescence or heavy use). It does not apply to assets such as cars nor does it apply to ships. The decision to de-pool must be made within two years of the year of acquisition.

Industrial buildings

The allowance is granted for expenditure on the construction of "industrial buildings" which are elaborately defined. Broadly the definition includes factories or buildings used for the purposes of a manufacturing trade or the subjection of goods to a process. Warehouses for the storage of goods which are to be used in manufacture are also industrial buildings, but warehouses used purely for distributive trades are not. An office is not normally an industrial building unless it is purely ancillary.

Enterprise zones

The government has established Enterprise Zones to encourage industry in areas suffering economic and physical decay. In such areas a 100% initial allowance can be obtained in respect of industrial *and* commercial buildings including offices and distributive warehouses. Exemption is also given from the uniform business rate (an annual local property tax).

Other allowances

Allowances are also available on ships, mines, oil wells and dredging.

(b) Trading losses

Trading losses for companies may be utilised as follows:

- set against total profits (both income and capital gains) of the same accounting period;
- set against total profits of the previous three accounting periods;
- carried forward and set off against future income from the same trade. There is no time limit on the carry forward;
- set against total profits within the same period of other companies within the same group (see (c) below).

(c) Group relief

In the case of a UK resident group (constituting a UK resident parent and UK resident subsidiaries which are 75% (whether directly or indirectly) owned by it), the losses and certain allowances and expenses of one company may be set off against the profits of another company in the same accounting period. A UK branch of a non-resident company does not qualify for group relief. Relief is also available between the members of a consortium and the consortium company, provided it is 75% owned by UK companies each owning at least 5% of the total share capital.

Trading losses can only be surrendered in the corresponding accounting period – there is no carry back or carry forward for group relief purposes.

(d) Pre-trading expenditure

Revenue expenditure incurred during the five years prior to the date of commencing a new trade is treated as though it was incurred on the day trading commenced, and is therefore allowable as a deduction in computing taxable trading income for that first year. Similarly, capital allowances on expenditure incurred prior to commencement of trade are available on the first day of trading.

(vii) **Chargeable gains**

(a) Computation

Corporation tax on chargeable gains arises on the disposal of an asset by a company. The chargeable gain is basically computed by deducting allowable expenditure from the consideration received on the disposal. Allowable expenditure includes the following items:

- the acquisition cost of the asset together with incidental expenses;
- expenditure incurred in enhancing the asset which is reflected in the state or nature of the asset; and
- the incidental costs of disposal.

To avoid taxation on paper gains this expenditure is adjusted to take account of increases brought about by inflation.

Capital losses may be set off against chargeable gains in the same period and carried forward against future gains, but they cannot be carried back, nor are they available for group relief.

(b) Roll-over relief

A company disposing of qualifying fixed assets used exclusively for the purposes of a trade, which expends the proceeds on other qualifying assets so used, may elect to roll-over (*i.e.* defer) chargeable gains arising on the old assets. It thereby obtains relief from tax on that gain, and must deduct the chargeable gain from the acquisition cost of the newly acquired assets. On a subsequent sale of the newly acquired assets, the chargeable gain arising is therefore increased by the gain on the old asset previously rolled over. This subsequent chargeable gain may itself be rolled over.

(viii) **National Insurance Contributions ("NIC")**

Contributions under the National Insurance Scheme go into a separate government fund used solely to pay for contribution-based benefits. Employees pay "primary contributions" ranging from 2% to 10% on earnings over a lower limit (£58 per week for the 1995/96 year of assessment). These are normally deducted by the employer under the Pay As You Earn system (see section headed Income Tax). In addition employers are liable for secondary contributions on the employee's total earnings once the above limit has been reached. Employer's contributions start at 3% for the 1995/96 year of assessment, and rise to 10.2% on earnings over £440 per week. In the case of employees there is an upper limit (£440 per week for 1995/96) beyond which they cease to be liable for further NIC, but there is no upper limit in respect of the employer's contribution.

Different rates apply to self-employed earners, and certain contributions are also payable on the business profits between lower and upper thresholds of an individual carrying on a trade.

(ix) **Uniform Business Rate**

There are no local taxes on income or profits. A local tax called Uniform Business Rate is levied by local authorities on the occupiers of non-domestic property. It is based on the annual rental value of the property and is charged at the rate of a number of pence in each £1 of that value. In 1995/96 the rate per £1 has been set at .432 pence. Apart from payments for specific services such as the supply of water, Uniform Business Rate is the only local tax paid by businesses in the United Kingdom.

(x) **Stamp duty**

Stamp duty is a tax on documents and is charged by reference to the price or value of the transaction embodied in the document. The main rate of duty is 1% charged on the conveyance or transfer of certain types of property including land. Leases are also subject to duty calculated by reference to the amount of rent and premium paid. Stamp duty is levied on share transfers at the rate of 0.5% of the price paid. Failure to stamp a document will render it inadmissible as evidence in the UK courts. A penalty of 5% per year is charged for late payment.

(xi) Personal taxation

(a) Income tax

Foreign nationals employed to work in the United Kingdom will generally be liable to UK income tax on all remuneration from that employment. Tax will normally be deducted by the employer according to a code issued by the Inland Revenue. This is known as the PAYE (Pay-As-You-Earn) system. Specific regard will be had to protection under an applicable double tax agreement as such a person, depending on the circumstances, may still be treated as resident or taxable in his own country. The terms of many agreements provide for "tie breaker" rules to determine residence.

Such a person's foreign investment income (*e.g.* dividends and gains) and remuneration for overseas duties under a separate employment is, however, taxable in the United Kingdom only if such sums are remitted to the United Kingdom for so long as he or she is not domiciled in the United Kingdom – that is, has not made his or her permanent home here.

The United Kingdom has one of the simplest systems of income tax in the world. In 1995/96 this consists of a lower rate of 20% on the first £3,200 of taxable income, a basic rate of 25%, and a single higher rate of 40% in respect of taxable income over £21,100; one of the lowest top rates of income tax in Europe.

If a foreign national works in Britain for 183 days or more in any tax year (6 April–5 April), or is otherwise regarded as resident for tax purposes, he is entitled to the basic personal allowances, currently £3,525 for 1995/96 for a single person, and an additional £1,720 for married persons – although relief at 20% is only given on this additional amount. There is also full tax relief on items such as pension scheme contributions.

Someone who is not domiciled in the United Kingdom, but works here for an overseas employer, may also be entitled to tax reductions for commitments at home – for example, payments of interest on certain loans to purchase a residence in the employer's home country where there is an overseas income out of which to make these payments. Relief is now limited to 20%.

Foreign nationals may well remain liable to overseas tax on their British earnings, but Britain's wide network of Double Taxation

Agreements will in most cases prevent the imposition of two sets of taxes.

Generous relief is given for travel expenses home incurred by expatriate (*i.e.* non-UK domiciled) employees working in the United Kingdom, for a period of five years from the date of their arrival in the United Kingdom. The relief enables employers to pay, or to reimburse, tax-free, the cost of travel by employees for an unlimited number of outward and return journeys between the home country and the United Kingdom. Relief is also available, subject to certain restrictions, for such travel by an employee's immediate family (spouse and children).

US citizens are in a special position because, unlike other countries, the USA taxes its citizens regardless of where they are resident. However, provided certain conditions are satisfied, they are able to exclude from US federal taxable income, up to $80,000 of UK earnings each year.

(b) Capital Gains Tax ("CGT")

CGT is computed in the same manner as chargeable capital gains for corporation tax purposes (see section (vii) (a) above). Individuals pay CGT at their top rate of income tax, but are entitled to an annual exemption of £6,000 per individual, which cannot be carried forward. Gifts to associated parties can attract CGT on the market value of the asset, although there are rules enabling the gain to be held over in certain cases. Non-UK residents are not liable to CGT.

(c) Inheritance Tax ("IHT")

IHT is a direct tax designed mainly to tax gifts on death. However, to prevent avoidance, lifetime gifts are only treated as potentially exempt until the donor survives seven years, and there are special rules where the donor does not fully dispose of the property and reserves a benefit. The charge is cumulative and takes account of all gifts made in any seven year period. From 5 April 1995, no tax is payable in respect of the first £154,000 and the rate of IHT is thereafter 40%. Gifts of certain assets, such as business property and unquoted company shareholdings, are effectively taxed at a lower rate and may even avoid tax altogether.

UK domiciled individuals are liable to IHT on all their property. Non-UK domiciles are liable to IHT in respect of UK property, but the position may be relieved by a double tax agreement. Property situated outside the United Kingdom will not be subject to IHT unless the non-UK domiciled individual has been UK resident in seventeen out of the last twenty tax years.

16. CUSTOMS DUTIES

Scope

Customs duty
Duty rates
Reliefs
Suspensory regimes
Transfer pricing

(i) Customs duty

(a) Background

Customs duty is the tax levied on goods imported into the European Community (EU) from "third countries" (that is, countries outside the EU). The basis of Community Customs' policy is the Customs Union. The prime feature of the Customs Union is that, for customs duty purposes, the EU is treated as one country, so that customs duty is not levied on goods traded between EU Member States. This means that the goods can be regarded as being in "free circulation" as long as they have either:

- originated in a Member State of the EU; or
- if they have been imported into the EU from a third country and all customs duties have been paid and all importation formalities have been finalised.

Practical point

If goods are imported into the United Kingdom, the importer must normally declare them by making an import entry and delivering it to Customs. The importer may either do it himself, or arrange for an agent to act for him. Certain approved traders and agents can input entry data direct to the Customs' computerised entry processing system: this is called Direct Trader Input.

There are a number of free trade agreements between the EU and various other countries. The EU is a member of the General Agreement on Tariffs and Trade ("GATT") and is expected to become a member of the World Trade Organisation. The EU consolidated existing Customs Legislation to create a Common Customs Code. The Code came into force on 1 January 1994 and applies throughout the EU, including the United Kingdom. As a result, Customs procedures, tariffs, clarifications, rules of origin and rates of duty are harmonised throughout the EU and should, in all cases, be the same in the United Kingdom as elsewhere within the EU.

Home produced goods are liable only to two charges, namely excise duty and VAT. Imported goods can be liable to four kinds of charges:

- customs duty (and anti-dumping duty);
- excise duty;
- agricultural levy; and
- VAT.

Customs duty is collected in the United Kingdom on behalf of the EU by HM Customs and Excise while excise duty and VAT go towards the UK national budget. Unlike VAT, customs duty is a "sticking tax", in that under most circumstances it is not a reclaimable cost, but sticks with the importer or his customer.

(b) Excise duty

Customs duty should not be confused with excise duty which is a separate tax levied on certain goods (for example alcoholic drink, tobacco and hydrocarbon oil) when produced in the United Kingdom or when imported into the United Kingdom. Excise duty is also charged on certain UK activities such as betting and gaming.

(c) Anti-dumping duty

Anti-dumping duties may be levied when an imported product is being sold in the EU at below the price of the product in its home market and this is causing injury to EU industry. An investigation and a formal decision is required before anti-dumping duties can be imposed. (See Chapter 14).

(d) Agricultural levy

Agricultural products may also attract separate import charges under the Common Agricultural Policy (CAP) of the EU.

(e) Value added tax

VAT is chargeable at a zero or 17.5% rate both on goods supplied in the United Kingdom, on goods acquired from another EU Member State, and on goods imported into the United Kingdom from a third country.

(f) Transaction value

The EU agreed to the Valuation Code of GATT. As a result, the primary basis of Customs' valuation is the "transaction value" of the imported goods.

The transaction value of goods (with certain adjustments) is the value on which the EU importer is required to pay customs duty. The transaction value is the invoiced price for the goods. However, when the invoice price cannot be used as the transaction value, other methods of valuation are used in the descending order set out below:

- a transaction value method previously accepted by Customs and Excise for goods identical to those being valued;
- a method based on a value previously accepted for goods which are similar to those being valued;
- a deductive method, which uses as a starting point the price at which the goods or identical or similar goods are sold in the EU;
- the computed value method, which is made up of the manufacturing costs of the imported goods plus an amount for profit and general expenses; and

- the fall back method, for use where the customs' value cannot be determined under any of the above valuation methods.

Each method is applied only when previous methods have been tried unsuccessfully, except, at the option of the importer, the order of two methods (deductive value method and computed value method) may be reversed.

(g) Calculating the transaction value

The following items (unless already included) must always be added to the price paid or payable for the goods when sold for export to an EU country.

- delivery costs *e.g.* costs of transport, insurance, loading or handling connected with delivering the goods to the EU border;
- commission, royalties and licence fees: this is by nature complex and it is recommended that the opinion of the Customs and Excise valuation branch is sought;
- the proceeds of resale, if they accrue either directly or indirectly to the sale of the goods;
- goods and services provided free of charge or at a reduced rate by the buyer, for example:
  - materials, components and similar items incorporated in the imported goods, such as price tags and labels;
  - tools, moulds and similar items used in producing the imported goods;
  - materials consumed in producing the imported goods such as abrasives and lubricants; and
  - engineering development, design work and plans carried out outside the EU and necessary for producing the imported goods.

The following items may be omitted from the value for duty if included in the price paid or payable, but evidence may be needed to support any claim to deductions made by the buyer:

- delivery costs within the EU;
- EU duties or tax;
- taxes believed already paid in the country of origin or export;
- trade, quantity or cash discounts;
- dividends;
- cost of marketing, advertising, promotion and guarantee or warranty services if carried out at buyers' expense;
- buying commission;
- interest charges payable under a financing agreement for buying the imported goods; and
- payments for the rights of reproduction if they are separately distinguished from the price paid or payable.

(ii) Duty rates

(a) Classification of goods

The rate at which customs duty is charged on import of goods into the United Kingdom and other Member States of the EU, is found by reference to the "Tariff". It is important to classify goods correctly to ensure that:

- the right amount of duty is paid;
- any special measures, for example, licenses and quotas are taken into account; and
- the right information is given to governments and statisticians.

The Tariff contains 97 Chapters and 15,000 sub-headings. Notes to the Tariff Sections, Chapters and sub-headings are designed to ensure that any product can only be classified in one place in the Tariff.

Since 1 January 1991, under EU rules, traders have been able to apply in writing to HM Customs and Excise for legally binding written classification decisions which remain valid for six years.

Practical point

Ensure goods are correctly classified to minimise the customs duty payable.

(b) Customs duty suspension

Within the Tariff there are numerous temporary suspensions and reductions of duty applying mainly to chemical and electronic goods or products. If products are imported because similar goods are not produced within the Community, the importer can apply for the product to be added to the list of duty suspensions.

(c) General valuation statement

Individual valuation declarations should normally accompany import entries for goods liable to customs duty, where the value exceeds £2,000. However, rather than complete a document in respect of each consignment, it is possible to save time and effort by completing and registering a general valuation statement. This form need only be completed once every three years, providing the terms or conditions of supply in that period do not change.

(iii) **Reliefs**

(a) Background

In order to assist certain industries and trades, some goods may be imported free, or at a reduced rate of Customs duty, on condition that they are used for prescribed purposes. This relief can apply to goods that are also eligible for a tariff quota or temporary suspension of duty, and therefore a decision must be made as to which relief it is most beneficial to claim. Goods which qualify for this relief are identified in the Tariff. Typical goods include civil aircraft and parts and equipment for them, parts for the manufacture of motor vehicles and materials for ships' construction and repair.

(b) Inward processing relief

Inward Processing Relief ("IPR") is the system by which goods imported from outside the EU for "processing" and subsequent re-export from the Community, may be relieved from Customs duties and from certain other charges. The term processing has a wide meaning as demonstrated below. The relief applies to:

- customs duties, including anti-dumping duties; and
- agricultural levies and other import/export charges under the CAP of the EU.

IPR does not generally extend to VAT, but the tax may not be paid at importation into the United Kingdom in respect of goods for repair, renovation, modification or certain treatment, providing:

- re-exported goods are identifiable as the imported goods;
- ownership of the goods is not transferred to the UK processor; and
- the processed goods are re-exported within six months.

There are two methods of obtaining relief under IPR. These are the suspension and the drawback methods. Under the suspension method, duty is not paid at importation, and is only payable if the goods or the products made from them (known as compensating products), remain within the EU. This is obviously the most advantageous method for cashflow purposes, but the goods must be intended for re-export and, if they remain within the Community and are put onto the home market, interest is due on the duty payable.

Under the drawback method, duty is payable on the goods at the time of importation and is claimed back from Customs after they have been re-exported to a country outside the EU. The drawback method cannot be used for any of the following imports:

- CAP goods;
- goods subject to quantitative import restrictions; or

- goods which might qualify for preferential arrangements within tariff quotas or allocated ceilings.

It is also a condition of using the drawback method that duty is reclaimed from Customs within six months of the date of export of the processed goods.

With the extension of the EU to include Austria, Finland and Sweden, goods which were in free circulation in these countries and placed under IPR or temporary importation before 1 January 1995 may, subject to proof, also be deemed to be in free circulation in the EU.

(c) Outward processing relief

Outward Processing Relief ("OPR") permits, subject to certain conditions, goods which are in free circulation or held under IPR to be exported from the EU for process or repair and re-imported wholly or partly free of Customs duty. If the goods are repaired in return for payment, Customs duty will be based on the charge made by the supplier. Where the goods are repaired free of charge for contractual or legal reasons, for example, under a guarantee or warranty, the reimported goods receive total relief from Customs duty. In all other circumstances, the relief is calculated by deducting the duty applicable to the exported goods from the duty due on the returned products.

OPR extends to Customs duty, agricultural and other CAP levies, but there is a similar relief for VAT subject to certain conditions.

Two other important points to note:

- authorisation must be obtained in advance, and sufficient time should be allowed for this; and
- it must be possible to identify the exported goods in the imported products.

(d) Other reliefs

There are a number of other Customs duty reliefs available, some of which are applicable to VAT, and many which are of a specialist nature. It is beyond the scope of this guide to describe them all but they include:

- returned goods relief, which allows exports from the EU to be wholly or partly relieved from Customs duty;
- rejected imports, where an importer discovers that the goods he has imported are defective, damaged or do not comply with the contract under which they were imported;
- temporary importation relief, which comprise additional reliefs from duty and/or VAT which are available in cases where goods are imported into the United Kingdom for temporary purposes only;
- reliefs on personal property;
- goods imported for examination, analysis or testing; and
- scientific or medical instruments and apparatus imported for non-commercial purposes, when goods of an equivalent nature are not available in the EU.

(iv) **Suspensory regimes**

(a) Background

If there is no tariff provision or applicable duty relief to avoid the payment of duty, it may be possible to delay the time at which the import charges have to be paid, by taking advantage of one of Customs' suspensory regimes – Customs warehousing, free zones, and the duty deferment system.

(b) Warehousing

If a business imports non-Community goods liable to customs duty and/or CAP charges, then it can place them in an approved warehouse. Whilst the goods are warehoused, the duty and import VAT do not have to be paid. Charges are usually payable when the goods are removed from the warehouse.

Practical point

Delay the payment of duty and VAT on the import of goods from outside the EU by holding the goods in a Customs approved warehouse.

(c) Free zones

Goods can be moved into a free zone without paying import charges (although relief from excise duty is available only if there is an approved excise warehouse in the zone). The importer pays duty and import VAT if the importer:

- brings goods out of the zone into the UK market; or
- uses or consumes them in the zone.

Within the zone, the importer may process imported goods free of Customs duty and import VAT except that:

- Customs duty is payable when products are intended for the United Kingdom or other EU markets; and
- import VAT is payable when processed goods are delivered for the UK market.

Free zones in the United Kingdom are currently operational at Liverpool, Birmingham Airport, Southampton, Tilbury, Prestwick and Humberside.

(d) Inland clearance depots (ICDs)

Instead of having the goods cleared at a port or airport, it may be easier to get Customs clearance at an approved inland depot. There are depots throughout the United Kingdom. Normally only goods in containers, rail freight wagons or road vehicles which can be sealed, may be removed for clearance inland. In some cases however,

Customs may allow the use of other means of conveyance which cannot be sealed.

(e) Duty deferment system

Using the duty deferment system, an importer can defer payment of VAT, Customs duty, CAP levies, anti-dumping duty, and excise duty, for an average of thirty days. With the exception of excise duty, payment for the import charges is made on the fifteenth day of the month following the date of importation or, if the goods are imported into a Customs' warehouse, the fifteenth day following removal of the goods from the warehouse to home use. For excise duty, the accounting period runs from the fifteenth of the month to the fourteenth of the following month, with payments made on the 29th of the month. Each month, the VAT, Customs duty and other charges due at importation are debited from the approved trader's bank account.

A guarantee from a bank or insurance company which has the approval of Customs & Excise is required.

(v) **Transfer pricing**

It is expected that the EU Convention on Arbitration in relation to transfer pricing disputes will be in force by February 1995. On 1 January 1994 the new European Community Customs Code came into force. In conjunction they will have serious implications for parents and subsidiaries. So far as a Customs' value is concerned it is necessary to translate sale and purchase into an appropriate currency. The Code provides that the rate of exchange shall be that duly published by the competent authorities of the member state. In the United Kingdom this means the period rate of exchange published weekly by Customs and Excise.

Article 29 of the Code recognises that there are cases in which the relationship between the exporter and the importer is not just that of buyer and seller – *i.e.* where they are related. The fact that the buyer and seller are related does not automatically override the presumption that the transaction value is the point of reference. It is necessary to look at the facts to work out whether the relationship has affected the price. If Customs take the view that the price has been affected then they must give the importer the opportunity to respond. The importer will then have to demonstrate that the transaction value closely approximates to sales of similar goods where there is no special relationship and the "computed" value of similar or identical goods.

If the importer cannot convince Customs that the transaction value represents an arms length price there are a number of criteria to be used in a set sequence in order to ascertain the required value, these criteria are:

- the transaction value of identical goods exported to the European Community at or about the same time;
- the transaction value of similar goods;
- the transaction value derived from the unit price at which identical or similar imported goods are sold within the EU; and
- the computed value. (This value is made up of the costs of materials, the cost of manufacturing processes and an amount for profit and general expenses.)

The aims of Customs and Excise and the Inland Revenue may conflict. Customs and Excise will generally seek to ensure that duty is paid on the highest acquisition value whilst the Inland Revenue may be seeking to argue the reverse (*i.e.* a lower importation price). There is no rule which provides that valuation accepted by one authority should automatically be accepted by the other, although Customs are legally entitled to pass information over to the Inland Revenue. The Customs' approach to valuation is probably more developed than that of the Inland Revenue, and it is a matter that the importer should not consider lightly. The method of establishing an arms length price for corporation tax purposes does not have the legislative background which is available to Customs and Excise.

17. VALUE ADDED TAX

Outline

The United Kingdom became an EU Member State on 1 January 1973 and was obliged to introduce VAT in accordance with its treaty obligations. The legislation in fact had already been enacted and came into force on 1 April 1973, although this was substantially amended to comply with the EU harmonising provisions effective from 1 January 1978, and was consolidated in the Value Added Tax Act 1983. It was further amended to comply with the single market provisions effective from 1 January 1993. The current VAT Consolidation Act, the Value Added Tax Act 1994, came into force on 1 September 1994.

The United Kingdom (comprising England, Scotland, Wales and Northern Ireland) is in a customs union. The Isle of Man introduced VAT under separate but almost identical legislation under the terms of the customs union. The two countries are treated as a single area for VAT purposes. The Isle of Man is also treated as part of the EU territory for EU purposes.

Scope

Taxable transactions
Credit mechanism
Taxable Persons
Exports
Tax returns

(i) Taxable transactions

VAT is a broadly based tax on consumer expenditure. It is a tax on three classes of transaction made in the United Kingdom.

(a) Supplies of goods and services

VAT is charged on supplies of goods and services made in the United

Kingdom by traders, *i.e.* individuals, partnerships and corporate bodies, referred to as "Taxable Persons". Tax is charged by the Taxable Person who makes the supply and who periodically pays the amount so charged to the Commissioners. This tax is known as "Output Tax".

(b) Events treated as a supply

A number of events which do **not** amount to a supply or do not meet the required conditions for tax to be charged on them are treated as if supplies for VAT purposes were made in the United Kingdom by Taxable Persons. Tax is accounted for to the Commissioners in the same manner as Output Tax. The one difference from supplies is that the "customer" is normally the Taxable Person himself and in such cases there is no onward charge to a third party.

(c) Imported or acquired goods

VAT is charged when (a) goods are imported into the United Kingdom from places outside the EU Member States and (b) acquired from another EU Member State.

The tax due on goods imported from third countries is paid direct to the Commissioners at the time of importation. This is normally the time when goods are entered for home use, either at the time of importation or when they are removed from a warehouse or a free zone. The rate of tax is the same as if the goods had been supplied in the United Kingdom (whether or not the person importing the goods is registered for VAT).

In the case of goods acquired from another European Member State, VAT will no longer be paid when the goods enter the United Kingdom. Instead, most transactions between VAT registered businesses will not bear VAT at origin; the supply will be subject to the UK rate of VAT and will be accounted for on the normal tax return. When the person importing is not registered for VAT, any goods purchased from a supplier in another EU Member State will bear VAT at origin.

Special rules apply to goods which were in the process of being imported into the United Kingdom from Austria, Finland and Sweden on 1 January 1995.

(ii) Credit mechanism

VAT is largely removed from business costs, and therefore confined to consumer expenditure, by providing Taxable Persons with a credit mechanism. Subject to a number of exceptions, Taxable Persons are entitled to recover the VAT they have paid from the Commissioners. This tax is known as "Input Tax" and represents:

- tax chargeable on goods and services supplied to them by other Taxable Persons;
- tax accounted for on events treated as supplies;
- tax paid to the Commissioners on goods imported from a third country; and
- tax accounted for to the Commissioners on goods acquired from another EU Member State.

VAT is removed from the business costs of overseas traders who are not taxable persons by a system of refund. Separate schemes apply for traders carrying on business in EU Member States and third countries. VAT is also removed from certain non-business expenditure. Certain goods and services supplied to specified persons are charged to tax at zero rate because of the character of the goods or services, or because of category of person to whom they are supplied. In addition, certain goods and services are exempted from tax, or VAT is chargeable on only part of the consideration passing on certain expenditure common to both business and private consumers.

(iii) Taxable Persons

A Taxable Person is someone who is, or is required to be registered for the purposes of VAT. A person is required to register if he makes taxable supplies or acquisitions and his taxable turnover exceeds the prescribed limits. A Taxable Person is also someone who registers voluntarily in other circumstances and is not exempted from registration. At present the threshold turnover requiring registration is £46,000. The current rate of VAT is 17.5%.

Practical point

A trader with taxable sales below the registration limits should consider voluntary registration. Whilst this would require VAT to be charged and accounted for on the taxable supplies made to customers, it also allows the trader to recover the VAT attributable to his purchases.

(iv) Exports

In very broad terms, goods and services supplied in the United Kingdom for consumption abroad are relieved from tax. A general relief is available for goods and a more restricted relief for services.

(v) Tax returns

A taxable person is required to account for any payable VAT by reference to prescribed accounting periods. The relevant prescribed accounting period varies depending on a number of circumstances, and can be one month, three months, or such other period as the Commissioners may determine in particular cases. In practice, one month periods are available to traders entitled to repayment of VAT other than those who register voluntarily.

A taxable person is required to furnish a tax return on the prescribed form in respect of each prescribed accounting period. Normally, a return must be furnished one calendar month after the end of the prescribed accounting period to which it relates.

The tax return should include the following information:

- tax due in the period on sales and other outputs;
- tax due in the period in respect of acquisitions;
- tax reclaimed in the period on purchases and other inputs; and
- the net amount of tax due or repayable by the Commissioners.

Practical point

Most foreign persons carrying on a business in the United Kingdom will need to register for VAT, and in respect of small operations will use the services of a local book-keeper to prepare their VAT returns.

The appointment of a book-keeper is also advisable to deal with and be responsible for the intricacies of the PAYE system governing payments to employees.

18. CRIMINAL AND CIVIL COURTS

Outline The English legal system, of which the English court structure is a part, is a common law system based on the recorded judgments of decided cases. This means that a body of law evolved initially through the system of precedent without reference to legislation passed by Parliament although recently that statute law has now become the primary source of law.

The court structure comprises civil and criminal jurisdiction. (The civil courts deal with dispute resolution in matters such as contract, torts (civil wrongs), property and public administration.)

Scope Criminal proceedings
Civil proceedings
Alternative dispute resolution

(i) Criminal proceedings

Criminal jurisdiction is generally exercised initially by Magistrates Courts, which also conduct committal proceedings in more serious matters to establish whether there is a case against the accused.

The Crown Court deals with serious offences once the accused has been committed for trial by the examining justices (magistrates). If the accused has pleaded not guilty, the trial takes place before a jury. The Crown Court also hears committals for sentencing from the Magistrates Court and hears appeals from that Court.

Appeal from the Magistrates Court also lies directly to a Divisional Court of the High Court. Cases on appeal from the Crown Court are heard by the Court of Appeal, Criminal Division, and then by the House of Lords.

(ii) Civil proceedings

Civil proceedings may be commenced either in the High Court or the County Court, and the choice will depend upon factors such as the monetary value of the claim and the complexity of the issue to be tried. The County Court (of which there are 320 in England and Wales) was intended originally to be a local court dealing with relatively minor civil litigation. Recent changes under the Courts and Legal Services Act 1990 have extended the limits on County Court jurisdiction and are expected to expand its workload enormously. The County Court is intended to offer a relatively inexpensive and reasonably fast procedure and it also has the facility for the arbitration of small claims at negligible cost.

The High Court is the senior court in which civil proceedings may be commenced. It has almost unlimited jurisdiction over civil proceedings and sits principally in London, but on the direction of the Lord Chancellor sits in other venues in England and Wales. It is split into three Divisions (Chancery, Queen's Bench and Family) and, except when sitting as a Divisional Court, it is usual for judges to sit alone.

The Magistrates Courts exercise a limited civil jurisdiction in domestic proceedings such as adoption, care and financial provision between spouses, and recovery of payments for water, gas, electricity and council tax.

Appeals from the County Court and from the High Court are heard by the Court of Appeal, Civil Division, which is presided over by the Master of the Rolls. It may sit anywhere in England and Wales but almost always sits in London.

The House of Lords is the upper House of Parliament, and as such is part of the legislature, but its Appellate Committee is the higher court of appeal. Appeals to the House of Lords are made from the Divisional Court of the Queen's Bench Division in some criminal matters and there are a small number of appeals direct from the High Court by means of the "leap-frog" procedure. These appeals are made on points of law of general public importance. When the United Kingdom joined the European Economic Community the House of Lords ceased to be the highest court of the English legal system. The European Court of Justice is the head of the new legal order created by the Treaty of Rome, and exercises a supervisory function by means of "interpretative references" rather than by a direct appeal mechanism.

Civil proceedings in the High Court are commenced principally by writ or summons which must be served on the defendant. The parties state their claims or defences by formal documents known as pleadings. The service of these pleadings is obligatory and subject to time limits. The process known as discovery compels a party to produce the relevant documents and seeks to ensure that no party is surprised by the evidence at trial. The court gives directions for the conduct of the proceedings so that all preparations have been made and witness statements and any expert evidence are exchanged before the trial begins. The procedure in the County Court is broadly similar.

In emergency situations an injunction, which is an order of the court which either compels a party to take a specified step or restrains him from so doing, can be obtained by immediate application to a judge without the presence of the other party. This is a short-term measure and the order given will not be in final form until there has been a full hearing with both parties present. Other types of interim relief are also available.

(iii) Alternative dispute resolution

The last decade has seen the growth of dispute resolution outside the court process. Arbitration has, of course, been available for a long time, but the use of *ad hoc* arbitrations as alternative dispute resolution (including mediation) has become more commonplace as parties wish to reduce both the costs of litigation and also publicity.

Practical point

The United Kingdom is the only country within the EU which has a legal system based on the common law which has made it the preferred forum for litigation for both the United States and former Commonwealth Countries.

INDEX